The Abomination of Desolation

According to the Prophet Daniel and Jesus Christ

By Brian Godawa

The Abomination of Desolation: According to the Prophet Daniel and Jesus Christ
1st Edition d

This is an excerpt from the appendix of the novel *Judah Maccabee – Part 2: Against the Gods of Greece.*

Warrior Poet Publishing
www.warriorpoetpublishing.com

ISBN: 978-1-963000-71-9 (eBook)
ISBN: 978-1-963000-91-7 (paperback)
ISBN: 978-1-963000-92-4 (Large Print)

Scripture quotations taken from *The Holy Bible: English Standard Version.* Wheaton: Standard Bible Society, 2001, unless otherwise indicated in the verse citation.

Other Bible versions cited:
NRSV: The Holy Bible: New Revised Standard Version (Nashville: Thomas Nelson Publishers, 1989).

LES: Rick Brannan et al., eds., The Lexham English Septuagint (Bellingham, WA: Lexham Press, 2012).

NASB95: New American Standard Bible, 1995 Edition: Paragraph Version (La Habra, CA: The Lockman Foundation, 1995).

Get the novel set
Judah Maccabee: Parts 1&2
based on the biblical research of this book you are reading.

 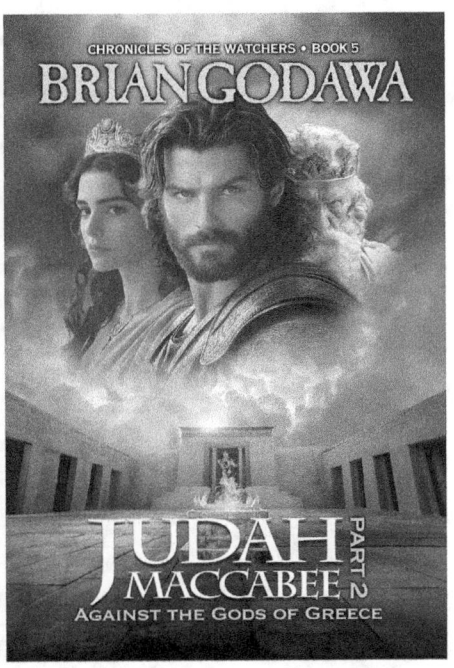

The Supernatural Story of Hanukkah and the Abomination of Desolation.

An epic action Bible novel about the most important Jewish story between the Old and New Testaments, the story of the Maccabees. Respected Christian author Brian Godawa reveals the spiritual realm like never before in this biblically faithful spiritual warfare novel.

https://godawa.com/get-judah-part-1/

(affiliate link)

Table of Contents

GET THE NOVEL SET *JUDAH MACCABEE: PARTS 1&2* 3

1 INTRODUCTION 5

2 THE PAST ABOMINATION OF DESOLATION 9

Antiochus IV Epiphanes 10

Antiochus and the Abomination of Desolation 14

Zeus and the Abomination of Desolation 24

Partial or Dual Fulfillment? 34

3 THE FUTURE ABOMINATION OF DESOLATION 42

Spoken of by Daniel 42

The Seventy Weeks 43

Titus Vespasian 52

Daniel 12 56

Jesus and the Abomination of Desolation 65

This Generation 65

Flee to the Mountains 69

Surrounded by Pagan Armies 70

What About the Image of the Beast? 74

Chart of the Syrian Wars in Daniel 11 75

GET THE NOVEL SET *JUDAH MACCABEE: PARTS 1&2* 80

GREAT OFFERS BY BRIAN GODAWA 81

ABOUT THE AUTHOR 82

The links in this book are my Amazon affiliate links.

1

Introduction

The abomination of desolation is a biblical term that is a part of eschatology, which is the study of "last things" in the Bible. Since one of the most common eschatological views propagated in Christian circles is premillennial dispensationalism, let's call it the Left Behind view for short (and who doesn't know about the mega-selling hit novel series *Left Behind*?). It conjures up fantastical supernatural scenarios in one's mind of a "rapture" of Christians out of this world, followed by an "Antichrist" who rises up as a world leader and makes a covenant with Israel, which he eventually breaks and sets up some kind of image of himself called "the abomination of desolation" in the Jewish temple in Jerusalem. The Antichrist makes it "come alive" and even speak. But eventually he requires Jews to worship it, which is the catalyst that wakens many of them up spiritually and leads to their turning toward Jesus Christ as their true Messiah. Jesus then returns to fight that Antichrist, destroy his allied nations, and set up his kingdom on earth.

Okay, I know that's only one interpretation of many that are out there. But I use it as one of the more popular examples of what is called "futurism," which is a broader term than the Left Behind view when applied to Bible prophecy. A futurist interpretation simply speculates that a specific Bible prophecy is yet to be fulfilled in *our* future. The belief that a Bible prophecy has already been fulfilled in the past is called a "preterist" interpretation. "Preterist" comes from the Latin word that means "past."

For example, all Christians are preterist in their interpretation of the Old Testament Bible prophecies of a coming Messiah to be born in Bethlehem to a virgin and who would be crucified for our sins because those are fulfilled in our past (preterist). But if you believe a certain

5

Bible prophecy is yet to be fulfilled in our future, such as a coming Antichrist, then you would have a futurist interpretation of that prophecy.

Sometimes the terms futurist and preterist are used in a summary way to refer to two dominant (though by no means monolithic) schools of thought about "last days" or "end times" prophecies. In general, futurists believe that there is an abomination of desolation (among many other things) to come in *our* future while preterists tend to believe that the abomination of desolation was fulfilled in our past *and only in our past*.

Like I said, there are so many views within each school of thought that I am sure some will quibble with various designations. But I am sure it will become clear that these are not the main issues to address on this subject.

To begin, let's take a look at all the places where the abomination of desolation shows up in Scripture. These are almost all in the book of Daniel and once in the Olivet discourse by Jesus, who is quoting Daniel. Notice that the exact phrase "abomination of desolation" is not always used. Sometimes it is described using the words or concepts of abomination and desolation together (bold underlines provided for focus).

> Daniel 8:11–14
> And the regular burnt offering was taken away from him, and the place of his sanctuary was overthrown.... "For how long is the vision concerning the regular burnt offering, the **transgression that makes desolate**, and the giving over of the sanctuary and host to be trampled underfoot?" And he said to me, "For 2,300 evenings and mornings. Then the sanctuary shall be restored to its rightful state."

Daniel 11:31
Forces from him shall appear and profane the temple and
fortress, and shall take away the regular burnt offering.
And they shall set up the **abomination that makes
desolate**.

Daniel 9:26–27
And the people of the prince who is to come shall destroy
the city and the sanctuary. Its end shall come with a flood,
and to the end there shall be war. **Desolations** are decreed.
And he shall make a strong covenant with many for one
week, and for half of the week he shall put an end to
sacrifice and offering. And on the **wing of abominations
shall come one who makes desolate**, until the decreed
end is poured out on the **desolator**."

Daniel 12:11
And from the time that the regular burnt offering is taken
away and the **abomination that makes desolate** is set up,
there shall be 1,290 days.

Matthew 24:15 (Mark 13:14)
So when you see the **abomination of desolation** spoken
of by the prophet Daniel, standing in the holy place (let the
reader understand)…

A cursory examination of all these verses show a common pattern
of elements or events that seem to overlap in creating a scenario. That
scenario includes the *tamid*, or daily sacrifice, in the temple being
"taken away" and the temple being "trampled underfoot," "profaned,"
or "destroyed." But what does this have to do with the abomination of
desolation?

Let's take a look at the words and concepts "abomination" and
"desolation" in their ancient context. The Hebrew word for
"abomination" is *siqqus*, which the *Theological Wordbook of the Old
Testament* describes as "always used in connection with idolatrous
practices, either referring to the idols themselves as being abhorrent and

detestable in God's sight or to something associated with the idolatrous ritual. Idols generally are referred to as an abomination (Jeremiah 16:18)."[1]

The god Chemosh is called "the abomination of Moab." Molech is "the abomination of the Ammonites." Ashtoreth is "the abomination of the Sidonians" (2 Kings 23:13). And so on.[2] The context of all the passages describing these abominations of the nations was physical idols (images) to which the pagan deities were linked.

The slight variation "transgression that makes desolate" (Daniel 8:14) is contextually about the same abomination. The Hebrew word for "transgression" means a crime that breaks relationship in some way.[3] So the idolatry that makes the temple desolate is a part of God's broken relationship with Israel.

The Hebrew word for "desolation" (*mesomem*) means to lay waste or make deserted.[4] This does not necessarily involve destruction. It carries the idea of desertion and is used of cities being deserted (Ezekiel 36:35) or the wasteland of the desert that represents a return to the precreation state of chaos (Ezekiel 33:28). So in the context of the temple, it most likely refers to being deserted of the presence of God or at least deserted of the rituals and practices of its purpose.

Put together and applied to the temple and/or city of Jerusalem, these words create the image of the presence of a pagan deity inside the temple of Yahweh that pollutes that temple and makes Yahweh leave its presence. Profanation is an intolerable violation of God's holiness, so he leaves that temple which has become host to a detestable abomination of idolatry.

---

[1] See also Ezekiel 5:11; 7:20; 2 Chronicles 15:8, etc. Hermann J. Austel, "2459 שָׁקַץ," in *Theological Wordbook of the Old Testament*, ed. R. Laird Harris, Gleason L. Archer Jr., and Bruce K. Waltke (Chicago: Moody Press, 1999), 955.

[2] See also Deuteronomy 29:17; I Kings 11:5-7; 2 Kings 23:24; 2 Chronicles 15:8; Isaiah 66:3; Jeremiah 7:30, etc.

[3] G. Herbert Livingston, "1846 פָּשַׁע," in *Theological Wordbook of the Old Testament*, ed. R. Laird Harris, Gleason L. Archer Jr., and Bruce K. Waltke (Chicago: Moody Press, 1999), 741.

[4] Willem VanGemeren, ed., *New International Dictionary of Old Testament Theology & Exegesis* (Grand Rapids, MI: Zondervan Publishing House, 1997), 167.

2

The Past Abomination of Desolation

Now that we have looked at the basic meaning of the term abomination of desolation, let's find out exactly how it is fulfilled in history. For the sake of clarity, I will announce my conclusion up front. There are so many different opinions on this matter that I want the reader to follow my argument without confusion or inaccurate assumptions.

Some interpret all the passages about the abomination of desolation to be talking about one and only one instance in history. Others add to that interpretation by suggesting that there is one concept of abomination of desolation that is repeated through history in partial fulfillments or multiple fulfillments. I will argue a third option, which is that Daniel is predicting exactly two separate abominations of desolation. The first one is in Daniel's near future when Antiochus Epiphanes erects an altar to Zeus in the Jerusalem temple in 168 BC. The second one is a similar offense in Daniel's distant future that mirrors Epiphanes but with significant differences.

So what about Jesus? What did he mean when he said, "So when you see the abomination of desolation spoken of by the prophet Daniel" (Matthew 24:15)? Jesus is referring to the second abomination. The first one had already happened in his past during the days of Antiochus Epiphanes. But the second one had not yet happened in his day. It was in his future.

Just who this second abomination is and when it occurs will be discussed below. But first let's see how the Daniel passages apply to the first abomination of desolation. To do so, we must get to know Antiochus IV Epiphanes.

Antiochus IV Epiphanes

The coming king foretold in Daniel's prophecy (Daniel 11:21-35) as a "contemptible" (ESV), "despicable" (NASB95), or "vile" person (NKJV) who would eventually bring about the "abomination of desolation" (v. 31) is also symbolized as "a little horn" that would grow out of Alexander's broken reign (Daniel 8:8-9) and grow powerful enough to defy Yahweh and oppress his holy people (8:9-14). That king would be the model and reflection of a future "little horn" that would also oppress God's people at a different time, the "time of the end" (Daniel 11:35, 40).[5]

That is why this story of the Maccabees is so important to the unfolding of God's plan to bring forth the Seed of the Woman that would crush the head of the Serpent—the very storyline of all three of my Chronicles series of novels (Genesis 3:15). That despicable and vile little horn was none other than Antiochus IV Epiphanes, the Seleucid king in Syria.

As 1 Maccabees says, Antiochus IV Epiphanes began to reign in the 137th "year of the Greeks," or about 175 BC. He was the youngest son of Antiochus III the Great, so he was not heir to the throne. He usurped the crown through political manipulation just as Daniel had prophesied.

> Daniel 11:21 (NASB95)
> A despicable person will arise, on whom the honor of
> kingship has not been conferred, but he will come in a
> time of tranquility and seize the kingdom by intrigue.

In order to understand the "intrigue" that Antiochus IV used to "seize" or usurp the crown, we must understand the historical situation of the time. The Republic of Rome would require the son of a king who

---

[5] The second "little horn" in Daniel 7:20-21, 24-25. The Beast of Revelation who matches that little horn of Daniel I found in Revelation 13:5-7; 17:9-10. For a full narrative depiction of this fulfillment, see my series, Chronicles of the Apocalypse.

was under their control to be held hostage in Rome in order to ensure the client king's compliance. As an Italian mobster might put it, "You get outta line, we gotta you son." Antiochus IV had the unfortunate circumstance to be one of those hostages when his father was king. But later, Antiochus used that hostage experience to his benefit. Commentator Robert Doran explains Antiochus IV's intriguing kingdom situation.

> After the Romans decisively defeated Antiochus III at the
> battle of Magnesia (190 BCE), this youngest son
> [Antiochus IV] was handed over to the Romans as a
> hostage. Antiochus III was succeeded in 187 BCE by his
> older son, Seleucus IV. Around 176, the Romans
> exchanged Antiochus [IV] for Seleucus IV's son
> Demetrius [because he was son of the new king]. On
> Seleucus IV's death in 175 BCE, Antiochus [IV] seized the
> opportunity to gain control of the kingdom in place of his
> brother's son.[6]

Some scholars believe Demetrius's death was too well-timed for Antiochus's rise not to have been an assassination. But Antiochus's previous stay in Rome was also fortuitous in educating him in the Roman way of politics and war. He would know his ultimate opponent well.

> Daniel 11:23
> And from the time that an alliance is made with him he
> shall act deceitfully, and he shall become strong with a
> small people.

As this prophecy indicates, Antiochus was in alliance with Rome because of their support for him when he came to power. But in 170 BC, Egypt demanded Coele-Syria back from Antiochus in a territorial

---

[6] Robert Doran, "The First Book of Maccabees," in *New Interpreter's Bible*, ed. Leander E. Keck, vol. 4 (Nashville: Abingdon Press, 1994–2004), 31.

dispute. Antiochus's capital city Antioch was in Coele-Syria, and he was not going to wait for such a personal attack to take place. So he consolidated his forces and invaded Egypt first in what would be called the Sixth Syrian War with King Ptolemy VI of Egypt in 169 BC.[7]

But Ptolemy could not stand against Antiochus. He was betrayed by his own advisors. Antiochus then swept in and took Ptolemy VI prisoner. But after he did so, the city of Alexandria installed Ptolemy's younger brother, Ptolemy VIII Euergetes II, to the throne. Angered by this affront, Antiochus plotted with his prisoner Ptolemy VI against the installed opponent by leaving and supporting Ptolemy VI as king in Memphis to counter Euergetes's claim. Eventually, the Ptolemy brother kings became allies and united over Egypt, which spoiled Antiochus's hopes of control.

Daniel foretold this all [my explanations in brackets].

> Daniel 11:25–28
> And he [Antiochus IV of Syria] shall stir up his power and his heart against the king of the south [Ptolemy VI of Egypt] with a great army. And the king of the south [Ptolemy] shall wage war with an exceedingly great and mighty army, but he shall not stand, for plots shall be devised against him. Even those who eat his food shall break him. His [Ptolemy's] army shall be swept away, and many shall fall down slain.
>
> And as for the two kings [Antiochus and Ptolemy VI], their hearts shall be bent on doing evil [plotting against Ptolemy Euregetes]. They shall speak lies at the same table, but to no avail [the Egyptian Ptolemy brothers unite], for the end is yet to be at the time appointed.

---

[7] The rest of this section on Daniel's prophecies fulfilled in Antiochus Epiphanes is drawn from Bruce W. Gore, *Historical and Chronological Context of the Bible* (Trafford Publishing, 2006), 10.19-23.

On his way back home to Syria, Antiochus decided to stop off in Jerusalem and plunder the temple for its treasury, described as imposing or "working his will."

> Daniel 11:28
> And he [Antiochus IV] shall return to his land with great wealth, but his heart shall be set against the holy covenant [Israel]. And he shall work his will and return to his own land [Syria].

This first invasion of Egypt by Antiochus IV was a high cost for the Seleucid king, who often pillaged temples as repositories of wealth to pay for his enterprises. Antiochus took the golden altar from the holy temple as well as the famous Menorah lamp stand and table of the Presence in addition to all the gold and silver temple utensils and any other hidden treasures he could find (1 Maccabees 1:20-23).

The prophet Daniel explains what would happen next. A year later in 168 BC, Antiochus decided to return to Egypt to finish what he had started and take the city of Alexandria. However, Rome would not tolerate this and sent an emissary, Caius Popilius Laenas, to put a stop to the Seleucid advance. This was the infamous incident where Popilius drew the line in the sand and told Antiochus to give him an answer of submission to Rome before he crossed it. If Syria did not pull back from Egypt, they would be at war with Rome. Not a cheerful prospect of victory. Here is how Daniel described it.

> Daniel 11:29
> At the time appointed he [Antiochus IV] shall return and come into the south [Egypt again], but it shall not be this time as it was before. For ships of Kittim [Rome] shall come against him, and he [Antiochus] shall be afraid and withdraw.

So Antiochus obeyed Rome and returned to Syria. But upon hearing of a possible uprising of Jews in Jerusalem, Antiochus became enraged and sent forces to the holy city to punish the Jewish insurgents and re-establish his authority over the region.

> Daniel 11:30
> And [Antiochus IV] shall turn back and be enraged and take action against the holy covenant [Israel/Jerusalem]. He [Antiochus] shall turn back and pay attention [favor] to those who forsake the holy covenant [Hellenist Jews].

See my chart at the end of this book about the fulfillment of Daniel 11 in the lead-up to and including the Syrian Wars of the second century BC.

Antiochus and the Abomination of Desolation

As Daniel describes above, Antiochus affirmed the Jews who had embraced Hellenism, but something inside him snapped against those Jews who did not. He decided to employ a violent strategy to end the religious freedom that the Jews had enjoyed since his predecessor, Antiochus III, had granted them autonomy.

On December 6, 167 BC, Antiochus IV stopped the daily Jewish sacrifices to Yahweh in the temple and set up an altar to the Greek god Zeus to replace those sacrifices to his patron deity. This was called by Daniel the "abomination of desolation" that profaned the temple.

> Daniel 11:31
> Forces from him [Antiochus] shall appear and profane the temple and fortress, and shall take away the regular burnt offering. And they shall set up the **abomination that makes desolate**.

The book of 1 Maccabees details the abominable desolation foretold by Daniel.

> 1 Maccabees 1:44–54 (LES)
> And the king [Antiochus IV Epiphanes] sent letters in the hands of messengers to Jerusalem and the cities of Judah, going after the customs of foreigners of the land, and to

withhold burnt offerings and sacrifice and drink offering from the sanctuary and to profane Sabbaths and festivals, and to defile the sanctuary and holy things.... And on the fifteenth day of Chislev, on the [one hundred and forty-fifth] year, **they built an abomination of desolation on the altar**.

More details on what the pagan worship of the abomination of desolation included are given later. But in short, the profaning involved not merely erecting a detestable idol but suppressing Jewish circumcision, dietary laws, and sabbaths while requiring sacrifices to Zeus with animals that the Jews considered unclean such as pigs.

The Hellenist Jews flattered the king by participating in the profane abomination of these demands, but others did not. Many would not stop circumcising their sons, worshipping on sabbaths, or refraining from eating pork and other unclean animals. And they would certainly not participate in sacrifices to Zeus. The result was the massive persecution and martyrdom of Jews by Antiochus described in the books of the Maccabees. Daniel prophesied the suffering and martyrdom as a refining fire of holiness.

Daniel 11:32–35
He [Antiochus] shall seduce with flattery those who violate the covenant [Hellenist Jews], but the people who know their God [holy Jews] shall stand firm and take action [disobey Antiochus's decrees]. And the wise among the people shall make many understand, though for some days they shall stumble by sword and flame, by captivity and plunder. When they stumble, they shall receive a little help [from the Maccabean uprising] ... and some of the wise shall stumble, so that they may be refined, purified, and made white, until the time of the end.

The family of Mattathias led by Judas Maccabeus not only refused to obey but stood in violent resistance and built an army of defiance. Their war against the Seleucid king ended with temporary victory in

165 BC, and Judas cleansed the Jerusalem temple of its abomination with a reinstatement of biblical sacrifices.[8]

Amazingly, Daniel foretold the amount of time this entire series of events would take: 2,300 days ("evenings and mornings").

> Daniel 8:13–14
> "For how long is the vision concerning the regular burnt offering, the transgression that makes desolate, and the giving over of the sanctuary and host to be trampled underfoot?" And he said to me, "**For 2,300 evenings and mornings**. Then the sanctuary shall be restored to its rightful state."

2,300 days comes out to about six years and three months (the "evening and morning" phrase may refer to the fact that the daily sacrifice was actually performed in the evening and in the morning of each day). The description of the sanctuary and host being "trampled underfoot" does not refer to physical destruction but to the polluting presence of pagan forces of idolatry occupying that temple. Commentator Jay Rogers explains this fulfillment.

> This is the time period, exactly six-years and three-and-a-half-months, during which Antiochus occupied the city of Jerusalem. Although the Jews were oppressed for over six years under the tyranny of Antiochus, for the last three years of the occupation, the sacrifices ceased to be offered.[9]

In all his defiance, the "little horn," Antiochus IV Epiphanes, did not thwart the will of God. But he had tried. This incident marks Epiphanes as one of the most infamous of villains in Jewish history,

---

[8] 1 Maccabees 4:36-61; 2 Maccabees 10:1-9.

[9] Jay Rogers, *In the Days of These Kings: The Book of Daniel in Preterist Perspective* (Clermont, FL: Media House International, 2017), 60. The 2,300 number could also represent a total of 1,150 days, each day of which included both morning and evening sacrifice. That would be approximately the three and a half years of the stopped burnt offerings. The result would be the same with a slight difference of perspective.

indeed in Christian history since he would become a template for another future ruler who would set up a second abomination of desolation in the Jerusalem temple. A pattern of historical repetition.

The two places where Daniel describes this second abomination of desolation are Daniel 9 and 12.

> Daniel 9:26–27
> And the people of the prince who is to come shall destroy the city [Jerusalem] and the sanctuary. Its end shall come with a flood, and to the end there shall be war. **Desolations** are decreed. And he shall make a strong covenant with many for one week, and for half of the week he shall put an end to sacrifice and offering. And on the **wing of abominations shall come one who makes desolate**, until the decreed end is poured out on the **desolate**."

> Daniel 12:7–11
> When the shattering of the power of the holy people comes to an end all these things would be finished. I heard, but I did not understand. Then I said, "O my lord, what shall be the outcome of these things?" He said, "Go your way, Daniel, for the words are shut up and sealed **until the time of the end**.... And from the time that the regular burnt offering is taken away and the **abomination that makes desolate** is set up, there shall be 1,290 days.

Though we read in these passages similar terminology of "abomination of desolation" related to the holy people, temple, and city as we saw in Daniel 8 and 11, we know for several reasons that these prophesies are not about Antiochus Epiphanes but about a future abominator. First, Antiochus Epiphanes polluted the temple but did not destroy it or the city of Jerusalem. The second abominator would make the temple "desolate" (Daniel 9:27) *and* destroy both the city of Jerusalem and the temple (9:26).

Second, the new abomination would occur at "the time of the end" and "when the shattering of the power of the holy people comes to an end." The era of the Maccabees was not the end of anything in relation to God's timeline of history since the power of the Jews did not come to an end but kept on with the success of the Maccabees. That power would only be shattered for good when the Roman Beast destroyed the temple totally and permanently in the generation of Messiah Jesus.

Third, the return to the regular burnt offering in the days of Antiochus was 2,300 days (Daniel 8:14), not the 1,290 days spoken of here in Daniel 12:11.

So what we see then in Daniel are two different abominations of desolation that are called by the same epithet or nickname phrase because they share a pattern of behavior in relation to God's people and temple. They both invade God's holy temple, they both stop the daily sacrifice, and they both desolate the temple with idolatrous presence for a time. But the second one does worse in destroying both temple and city. At this point readers may want to engage in speculation as to who this new "prince" is and when he will arise in history. I have addressed that separate issue later in this book. For now, I want to continue with an exploration of the character of Antiochus IV Epiphanes as described by Scripture and history.

One aspect of that character is another repeating pattern of behavior in the kings of the "beastly" Gentile kingdoms: god-like pride. Arrogant ancient rulers always seem to want to overthrow God and take his place.

> Daniel 8:25
> And he [the little horn-Antiochus] shall even **rise up
> against the Prince of princes**, and he shall be broken—
> but by no human hand.

The phrase that Daniel uses to indicate the idolatrous arrogance of Gentile rulers involves derivations of "do as he wills." In Hebrew, do (*asah*) as he wills (*rason*). It carries the meaning of "doing what he pleases" as if the king was so great that like a god he could do whatever he wanted without resistance.

Daniel's first use of the phrase applies to King Cyrus the Great of Persia, who "*did as he willed* and became great. And there was no one who could rescue from his power" (Daniel 8:4). Daniel later describes Alexander the Great as "a mighty king who shall rule with great dominion and *do as he wills*" (11:3). After him comes Antiochus III the Great who would "*do as he wills* and none shall stand before him" (11:16).

The last king of which Daniel uses the phrase is one who would come "at the time of the end" of these kingdoms. This king would also "*do as he wills*" by "exalting himself and magnifying himself above every god and shall speak astonishing things against the God of gods" (Daniel 11:36). But this last willful king is not Antiochus IV Epiphanes because Antiochus was not the king *at the time of the end*. We will discuss who this king might be later. Let's stay with our focus on Epiphanes.

The willful king phrase takes an ironic twist when considered in its context of God, the king over all the earth, describing his sovereign predestination of their exact actions in history that would lead up to the finishing of the "transgression of Israel" against Yahweh (Daniel 11:36) through the coming of Messiah (Daniel 9:24). These kings all believed and behaved as if they were gods. But in the end, they were mere instruments in the true God's plans.

Antiochus Epiphanes is the only king in these chapters not referred to as "doing as he wills." Some English translations of Daniel 11:28 say that Antiochus "shall do as he will," but this is not in the Hebrew. It only says that he will act (asah) against the holy covenant. I.e., the first half of that phrase without the second willful component. Perhaps this is God's most demeaning and mocking gesture of all in avoiding even acknowledging the will of the "despicable" monster who profaned

Yahweh's house with the abomination of desolation. He's just another axe in the hand of God chastising his people (Isaiah 10:5, 15).

That said, contextually Antiochus was certainly in the line of kings who acted with godlike pretensions. In another prophecy, Daniel details this blasphemous arrogance of Antiochus Epiphanes against Yahweh and his people and heavenly host.

> Daniel 8:9–11
> Out of one of them came a little horn [Antiochus Epiphanes], which grew exceedingly great toward the south, toward the east, and toward the glorious land [Israel]. It grew great, even to the host of heaven. And some of the host and some of the stars it threw down to the ground and trampled on them. It became great, even as great as the Prince of the host [Angel of Yahweh].

Could a mere human king actually be capable of casting angels of the heavenly host to the ground?[10] Could he really rival the greatness of the highest Prince of the heavenly host, the Angel of Yahweh himself?[11] In the context of the Scriptures, obviously not. Humans in the presence of real heavenly beings often tremble in deathly fright. These words are more likely a reflection of the little horn's blasphemous words of arrogance in the face of God. Something that history bears out and Daniel interprets just a few verses later as "in his own mind he shall become great…. He shall even rise up against the Prince of princes, and he shall be broken—but by no human hand" (8:25).

---

[10] Stars are often symbols or representatives of elohim/gods/angels in the Bible and other Ancient Near Eastern literature, including Intertestamental Jewish literature. See my explanation of this literary symbolism in Brian Godawa *When Watchers Ruled the Nations: Pagan Gods at War with Israel's God and the Spiritual World of the Bible* (Texas: Warrior Poet Publishing, 2021), 29-37.

[11] There are two strong possibilities for understanding "The Prince of the host." He is either Michael the archangel or Yahweh himself, Jesus in preincarnate form. For Michael the archangel, see Brian Godawa, *When Watchers Ruled the Nations: Pagan Gods at War with Israel's God and the Spiritual World of the Bible* (Texas: Warrior Poet Publishing, 2021), 314-317. For the Angel of Yahweh as the Prince of the host, see Michael S. Heiser, *Angels: What the Bible Really Says about God's Heavenly Host* (Bellingham, WA: Lexham Press, 2018), 71–72.

The epithet "Epiphanes" that Antiochus IV took meant "manifest god," a true affront to the only creator God Yahweh. This delusional surname expressed his tyrannical behavior and reflected a madness that eventually inspired a satirical twist of the word Epiphanes into "Epimanes," which meant "utterly mad" or "madman."[12]

Roman historian Polybius wrote of Antiochus fancying himself a god come down to men by wandering around town in royal garb or plebian disguise to discuss technical matters of the arts and crafts with goldsmiths and jewelers. He would engage in drinking bouts in the taverns with a couple of his trusted advisors, Heraclides and Timarchus of Miletus. He would bestow godlike excessive gifts of ointments, food, or money upon unwitting strangers in the streets, sometimes out of the blue, sometimes in response to overheard desires.[13]

But his unpredictable acts of caprice could have their sinister side as well for as historian Edwyn Bevan warns, beware the caresses of a panther. "He felt no difficulty in pleasantries with the man at whom he designed to strike."[14]

Roman historian Livy wrote that Antiochus would also adjudicate on the most trivial of legal matters as if divinely omniscient, then move on to petty common interactions with a rather short human patience. In Antioch, he spent extravagantly on religious and civic splendor. He began building the magnificent temple of Olympian Zeus, which was gilded with gold throughout, and splurged on Greek theaters and Roman gladiator arenas.[15]

Of all the Greek deities, Antiochus favored Zeus. Not only did the king build the Antioch temple dedicated to that Supreme Deity but had

---

[12] John Whitehorne, "Antiochus (Person)," in *The Anchor Yale Bible Dictionary*, ed. David Noel Freedman (New York: Doubleday, 1992), 270.

[13] Polybius, *Histories* XXVI https://penelope.uchicago.edu/Thayer/E/Roman/Texts/Polybius/26*.html

[14] Edwyn Robert Bevan, *The House of Seleucus* (London, Edward Arnold Publishing, 1902), 129-130.

[15] Livy, Books XL-XLII With An English Translation, ed. Evan T. Sage and Alfred C. Schlesinger, *Ab Urbe Condita (Foster-Moore-Sage) English Text* (Medford, MA: Cambridge, Mass., Harvard University Press; London, William Heinemann, Ltd., 1938), 249–251.

previously built a vast temple of "Zeus Olympius" in Athens. He also put the storm god's face on newly minted coins in his realm. There are some grounds to believe that Antiochus identified himself with Zeus as the king of the gods.[16]

Ironically, most scholars agree that Antiochus did not originally have a particular animosity toward the Jews. Despite this ostentatious display and public dedication to Zeus, Antiochus himself was quite without religion. As Barry explains:

> His devotion to the worship of Zeus was but part of his idea
> that there be, instead of divers local and tribal faiths, a formal
> state religion, to become a powerful unifying factor, as a
> means of giving securer basis of solidarity to his empire.[17]

The king's imposition of Hellenism was that attempt to unify the empire through the transcendence of deity and religion. In a sense, he was playing with fire, the fire of true believers that he could not understand.

The death of Antiochus Epiphanes has more than one narrative in the books of the Maccabees. In 1 Maccabees 6, the Seleucid king is in Persia unsuccessfully seeking to plunder the city of Elymais to increase his waning wealth. A messenger tells Antiochus of Lysias's defeat to Judas Maccabeus in the battle of Beth-Zur and the subsequent cleansing of the temple, whereupon the king becomes physically sick with disappointment. A sickness that he believed would kill him. Pondering his deathbed, he painfully regrets his poor treatment of the Jews but doesn't repent so much as suffer spiritual punishment for his choices. He then appoints a regent over his young son until he is of age to reign. Then Antiochus dies. The writer wants to console himself that the king experiences some kind of justice in this world before he dies.

---

[16] Bevan, *The House of Seleucus*, 150.

[17] Phillips Barry, "Antiochus IV, Epiphanes," *Journal of Biblical Literature*, Vol. 29, No. 2 (1910), pp. 126-138

In 2 Maccabees 9, a different and more interesting tale is told with no less a religious agenda and a far greater hunger for earthly judgment. Antiochus is in Persepolis, Persia, seeking to rob its temples and gain control. He fails and retreats to Ecbatana near Babylonia, where he receives a message of Seleucid defeats to the Maccabees but *before* the cleansing of the temple has occurred.

Antiochus becomes so angry he leaves for Jerusalem, shouting in arrogance, "When I get there, I will make Jerusalem a cemetery of Jews" (9:4). We are then told that God in his providential retribution strikes the king with "a pain in his bowels, for which there was no relief, and with sharp internal tortures—and that very justly, for he had tortured the bowels of others with many and strange inflictions" (9:5-6). This does not stop Antiochus from his journey of rage. In fact, he tells his chariot driver to go faster. Unfortunately, the king falls out of the vehicle, and "the fall was so hard as to torture every limb of his body" (9:7).

In a verbose display of literary poetic justice, the writer mocks the king's epithet of "god manifest" by saying that he who once thought he had the "power of God manifest to all" was now "swarmed with worms" with an "intolerable stench" from the "rotting of his flesh." The storyteller really wants Antiochus to suffer deeply in this life for the pain he has caused as otherwise the Jewish suffering would seem without just recompense.

But Antiochus is enlightened and expresses his regret, not unlike King Nebuchadnezzar's revelation in the wild: "It is right to be subject to God; mortals should not think that they are equal to God" (9:12). Still, the writer does not want Antiochus to have the full release of forgiveness so he reminds us that even though the king made a vow to God to free the Jews from persecution and return the wealth he had stolen from the temple, "the Lord would no longer have mercy on him" (9:13).

Antiochus then appoints his son to take the throne. The writer concludes, "So the murderer and blasphemer, having endured the more intense suffering, such as he had inflicted on others, came to the end of his life by a most pitiable fate, among the mountains in a strange land" (9:28).

Abominable. Miserable. His flesh rotting. His bowels swollen with worms. His suffering unabated. In summary, the reader of 2 Maccabees can safely say of Antiochus Epiphanes, "Good riddance."

So we have come to understand the man behind the first abomination of desolation. Now, let us look at the detestable thing itself to see what it is.

Zeus and the Abomination of Desolation

Though there are many different versions of Greek mythology, the poet Hesiod (circa 700 BC) and his book *Theogony* is one of the foremost references for the origins, identities, and stories of their gods.[18] In it, we see a succession narrative of early gods overthrown by later gods.

In Greek mythology, first there was Chaos and Gaia (earth) with Night and Day. Ouranos (sky) and Gaia (earth) birthed the first set of primordial gods called the Titans. One of those Titans, Kronos, ambushed Ouranos, castrated him, and separated him (sky) from Gaia (earth), their version of a common component in most creation stories, the separation of heaven and earth.[19]

Kronos then took over and mated with his sister goddess Rhea. They gave birth to three female deities, Hestia, Demeter, and Hera, and three male deities, Hades, Poseidon, and Zeus. Because Kronos did not

---

[18] Other main sources of Greek mythology used by scholars that vary in some of their details are Homer, Orpheus, Apollodorus, Pausanius, and Greek historians such as Herodotus, Diodorus Siculus, and Plutarch.

[19] Hesiod, trans., Barry B. Powell, *The Poems of Hesiod: Theogony, Works and Days and the Shield of Herakles* (Oakland, CA: University of California Press, 2017), *Theogony* 95-145, pp 36-41.

want to be overthrown by his offspring as he had overthrown his own father, he swallowed his children.

Rhea, however, tricked Kronos and got him to swallow a stone wrapped in swaddling clothes instead of the real Zeus. Zeus grew up and managed to get Kronos to vomit Zeus's siblings into the world. Along with these freed captives are several Cyclopes, one-eyed monsters, who then provided the powerful weapon of thunderbolts to Zeus, a magical helmet of invisibility to Hades, and a mighty trident to Poseidon.[20] The mountain Olympus became their home.

Zeus and the twelve Olympians defeated Kronos and the other Titans in the Titanomachy and imprisoned them in Tartarus, after which Zeus took his place as king of the gods and was allotted the sky as his domain. He became known as a storm god with the epithet "Cloud-Gatherer."[21]

Though most people know about Zeus taking his sister goddess Hera as his wife, they may not be aware that Hera was his seventh and last wife. Nor was Zeus satisfied with only seven wives. He also took many mistresses, both goddess and human. Zeus was a randy, promiscuous adulterer. He became known for fathering many gods such as Apollo the sun god, Ares the god of war, and Athena goddess of war. He also mated with mortal women to birth human/god hybrids, the most famous of which was Heracles.

There is little doubt that Zeus's sexual interaction with humans was modeled on the ancient Near Eastern narrative of the divine Sons of God mating with human daughters of men. Though Heracles was not a giant like the human/angel hybrid Nephilim, he was certainly in the category of the Hebrew *gibborim*, the mighty men of old, the men of renown (Genesis 6:4). His character reflected the excess of a demigod as well.

---

[20] Apollodorus, *Library of Greek Mythology* 1.1.5-2.1 pp 27-28.
[21] Homer, *Illiad* 1.511.

He had extraordinary strength and extraordinary passions, including many sexual conquests of both men and women.

Like father, like son.

When Antiochus Epiphanes set up the "abomination of desolation" in the Jerusalem temple, he renamed it the temple of Zeus Olympian (2 Maccabees 6:2). But what did the abomination look like and what rituals did the king demand from the Jews? To answer that, we begin with the text of the Maccabees. 1 Maccabees is the least detailed. It simply states:

> 1 Maccabees 1:54-55 (LES)
> Now [the Seleucid officials] built an **abomination of desolation** on the [Jerusalem] altar, and in the cities around Judah, they built altars. And at the windows of their houses and in the streets, they burned incense.

> 1 Maccabees 1: 44-47 (LES)
> And the king [Antiochus] sent letters by messengers to Jerusalem and the towns of Judah; he directed them … to build altars and sacred precincts and shrines for idols, to sacrifice swine and other unclean animals.

Ancient Jewish historian Josephus wrote, "And when the king had built an idol altar upon God's Altar, he slew swine upon it, and so offered a sacrifice."[22]

In Hebrew, the word "abomination" (*siqqus*) was a word used in the context of physical images of pagan gods (idols) that Yahweh considered detestable in his presence.[23] The Hebrew word for "desolate" (*mesomem*) reinforced that alienation. It meant to make uninhabitable, thus implying the withdrawal of God's presence due to the presence of the abominable idol. Yahweh simply did not tolerate the worship of any gods before him (Exodus 20:3).

---

[22] Josephus, Antiquities 12.4 (253) Flavius Josephus and William Whiston, *The Works of Josephus: Complete and Unabridged* (Peabody: Hendrickson, 1987), 324.
[23] Deuteronomy 29:17; 2 Kings 23:24; 2 Chronicles 15:8; Jeremiah 13:27; 16:8; 32:34; Ezekiel 20:7; 32:23.

So the Hebrew conception in the words "abomination of desolation" involved the presence of the image of a false god. Desolation did not require actual destruction of the temple but simply religious pollution of images/idols that resulted in God's presence being withdrawn.

Josephus wrote that "the king [Antiochus Epiphanes] built an idol altar upon God's altar,"[24] which echoes 1 Maccabees 1:59: "They were sacrificing on the altar [to Zeus] that was on [Yahweh's] altar for burnt sacrifices." We are told nowhere what the idol altar built upon Yahweh's altar may have looked like. Most assume the simple description of new stones placed upon the existing stones of the Jerusalem altar. But why would there be a need to add additional stones to an existing functioning altar? Unless they were adding something distinctly Greek to that altar.

The implication is that the stones may have been actual idol images of some kind as those indicated by the Hebrew terms defined above. Though we know the Jerusalem temple was renamed for Zeus Olympian by Antiochus Epiphanes, we also know that altars to Zeus could include his image as well as those of other deities such as Athena.[25] A common ancient view of the abomination of desolation was that of Roman philosopher Porphyry (AD 234-305), who suggested that it was an actual statue of Zeus enthroned on the altar.[26] Such large statues of Zeus were known in other Greek conquered cities. Ancient historians wrote of a golden statue of Zeus 12 cubits (18 feet) high in the precinct of the Babylonian temple, a 40-foot-tall golden statue of Zeus at the temple of Belus, and a 72-foot-tall bronze statue of Zeus at Tarantum.[27]

---

[24] Josephus, *Antiquities* 12.5.4 [12.253].

[25] This is the case with the famous altar of Zeus at Pergamum that includes Athena.

[26] John Collins and Peter W. Flint, Ed., *The Book of Daniel: Composition and Reception Volume 2* (Boston, MA: Brill, 2001), 677.

[27] James Alan Montgomery, *A Critical and Exegetical Commentary on the Book of Daniel* (Edinburgh, T&T Clark, 1959), 193-194.

While the possibility of a statue on the altar has been rejected by more recent interpretations, it would make sense to place such a statue of Zeus into the Holy of Holies because that inner sanctuary was supposed to be the throne of God, with the ark of the covenant as his footstool. Such an act would represent Zeus taking over Yahweh's throne.

The Anchor Bible Commentary suggests the "abomination of desolation" may have consisted of three meteorite cult-stones (*massebot*) that represented the God of the Jews [Yahweh/Zeus], his female divine consort the Queen of Heaven [Anat/Athena], and his divine son [Dionysus].[28] Though entirely speculative, this would synchronize well with the idol worship of cult standing stones (*massebot*), already long practiced by the Jews historically.

Though the Jews would not have required cult-stones to be meteorites,[29] the Greek king would find commonality with massebot in the fact that the famous temple of Apollo at Delphi housed the Omphalos, a large meteorite conical stone that was believed to have been placed at that location by Zeus to mark it as the "navel" or center of the earth.[30]

Since it is likely the high priest Menelaus would have counseled Antiochus in this matter, Menelaus might have suggested a subversive way of syncretizing the gods of Canaan with the gods of Greece. Zeus had already been worshipped in Syrian cities as Ba'al-Shamem, and his consort was Anat (Athena). So massebot standing stones that represented gods interchangeable between Canaan and Greece might be one way of seeking the smoothest transition.

---

[28] Jonathan A. Goldstein, *I Maccabees: A New Translation with Introduction and Commentary, vol. 41*, Anchor Yale Bible (New Haven; London: Yale University Press, 2008), 224.

[29] "Standing Stones," Brian Godawa, *The Spiritual World of Jezebel and Elijah* (Texas: Warrior Poet Publishing, 2021), 97-99.

[30] Robin Hard, *The Routledge Handbook of Greek Mythology, 8th edition* (Oxon, OX: Routledge, 1928, 2020), 136-137.

But a strong argument against this massebot view is that Antiochus was extremely hostile to the Jewish religion and sought to deny them their distinctives in Torah, so it would not be as likely that he would seek a syncretistic blending as opposed to an explicit and hostile replacement of deities.[31]

Though an attempt to decode this nefarious abomination of desolation leaves us with a plethora of questions and unproven possibilities, it remains a fascinating subject for fictional speculation in the novel Judah Maccabee.

Regarding the activities of idolatry imposed by Antiochus, 2 Maccabees describes in more detail the imposition of Greek gods upon the Jews (bold emphasis added).

> 2 Maccabees 6:1-6 (RSV)
> Not long after this, the king sent an Athenian senator to compel the Jews to forsake the laws of their ancestors and no longer to live by the laws of God; **also to pollute the temple in Jerusalem and to call it the temple of Olympian Zeus, and to call the one in Gerizim the temple of Zeus-the-Friend-of-Strangers, as did the people who lived in that place**.
>
> Harsh and utterly grievous was the onslaught of evil. For the temple was filled with debauchery and reveling by the **Gentiles, who dallied with prostitutes and had intercourse with women within the sacred precincts**, and besides brought in things for sacrifice that were unfit. The altar was **covered with abominable offerings that were forbidden by the laws**. People could neither keep

---

[31] Bible scholar Johan Lust concludes, "These passages seem to identify the 'abomination of desolation' with an 'idol altar,' a kind of superstructure built upon the altar of the Lord. No mention is made of a statue of a pagan deity, nor of meteorites." Johan Lust, "Cult Sacrifice in Daniel. The Tamil and the Abomination of Desolation," John J. Collins and Peter W. Flint, Eds., *The Book of Daniel: Composition and Reception Volume 2* (Boston, MA: Brill, 2001), 684.

the sabbath, nor observe the festivals of their ancestors,
nor so much as confess themselves to be Jews.

After this, the writer of 2 Maccabees adds that at a festival for Dionysus, the Greek god of bacchanalia, the Jews were also forced to wear "wreaths of ivy and to walk in the procession in honor of Dionysus" (6:7). What the writer is too diplomatic to describe is that the procession of the festival, called the Dionysia, involved carrying large wooden or bronze "phalloi," images of phalluses on poles. A cart with a huge phallus image was pulled behind.

This is because the origin of the celebration was rooted in a mythical incident where the city of Athens rejected a gifted statue of Dionysus, so the god had sent a plague on the genitals of the male citizens. Their epidemic malady was only healed by the acceptance of the cult of Dionysus.[32]

But back to Zeus.

According to 2 Maccabees, the pagan worship of Zeus involved temple prostitutes in the sacred precincts of the temple mount. But again, this behavior was already well-known in Israel's history of Canaanite idol worship, so it would be another familiar addition to the imposed apostasy.

But the focus of worship was an idol altar built upon the Jerusalem altar of burnt offerings upon which unclean animals such as pigs were sacrificed. This idolatrous altar was considered the "abomination of desolation" predicted by the prophet Daniel.

---

[32] "Dionysia," Wikipedia: https://en.wikipedia.org/wiki/Dionysia
"The date of the desecration of the temple in the month just before the winter solstice (Kislev) may have coincided with a festival of Dionysus. Antiochus IV's Athenian expert may have suggested imposing on the Jews the "rustic Dionysia," which in Athens were celebrated in the month of Posideon=Kislev; indeed, the author at I 1:54–55 stresses that the rites were observed in the country towns." Jonathan A. Goldstein, *I Maccabees: A New Translation with Introduction and Commentary*, vol. 41, Anchor Yale Bible (New Haven; London: Yale University Press, 2008), 155.

Daniel 11:31
Forces from him [Antiochus Epiphanes] shall appear and
profane the temple and fortress [in Jerusalem], and shall
take away the regular burnt offering. And they shall set up
the **abomination that makes desolate**.

This same abomination of desolation is implicated in another
prophecy of Daniel that foretells the Maccabean incidents. And this one
brings in the spiritual powers involved in the incident.

Daniel 8:9–13
Out of one of them came a little horn [Antiochus
Epiphanes], which grew exceedingly great toward the
south, toward the east, and toward the glorious land. It
grew great, even to the host of heaven. And some of the
host and some of the stars it threw down to the ground and
trampled on them. It became great, even as great as the
Prince of the host. And the regular burnt offering was
taken away from him, and the place of his sanctuary was
overthrown. And a host will be given over to it together
with the regular burnt offering because of transgression,
and it will throw truth to the ground, and it will act and
prosper. Then I heard a holy one speaking, and another
holy one said to the one who spoke, "For how long is the
vision concerning the regular burnt offering, the
transgression that makes desolate, and the giving over
of the sanctuary and host to be trampled underfoot?"

As explained earlier, this little horn is a descendant of the great
single horn of the goat that represented Alexander the Great of
Macedon. After the Greek conqueror's death, his kingdom was divided
between four of his generals. Out of one of those generals, Seleucus,
came this little horn, Antiochus IV Epiphanes.

Those who would seek to find a mere earthly historical narrative
here see Antiochus growing so great and specifically with regard to the
"glorious land" of Israel that he would overcome the "Prince of the

host," interpreted as the high priest, from whom the regular burnt offering would be taken. A host of Jews would then be "given over to" Antiochus in both war and slavery. Antiochus then tramples the temple and God's people underfoot.

But this earthly naturalistic interpretation does not take into account the supernatural context that includes the spiritual powers at war in the heavenlies.

First, the context of this prophecy within the book of Daniel is quite supernatural. The chapter before it, Daniel 7, charted out the four Gentile kingdoms ending in Rome which culminate in the ascension of the Son of Man (Jesus) to his throne in heaven. We read of "ten thousand times ten thousand" who stood before that fiery throne as "the court sat in judgment" (Daniel 7:10). This phrase is always used of Yahweh's heavenly host of divine beings that surrounds him, often in judgment.[33]

So when Daniel 8:10-11 refers to the little horn Antiochus Epiphanes becoming "as great as the Prince of the host," this is not a mere reference to a human high priest but likely a supernatural reference to the godlike pretensions of Antiochus Epiphanes ("god manifest") in taking over Yahweh's house (the temple of his presence) and with it the spiritual authority over Israel.

In Daniel, the Aramaic word for "prince" (*sar*) is used of spiritual princes over nations (Daniel 10:13, 20-21). Daniel interprets for us later in the passage that Antiochus becoming "as great as the Prince of the host" was another way of saying that the little horn "shall rise up against the Prince of princes," that "in his own mind he shall become great" (8:25). In fact, he would not be a god but "he shall be broken—but not by human hands" (8:25). This was spiritual warfare with historic consequences. There is only one Prince of princes in both heaven and earth, and that is Yahweh.[34] And there is only one Prince of the host,

---

[33] Jude 14:15; Psalm 68:17; Revelation 5:11; Deuteronomy 33:2-3 LXX.
[34] "Prince of the host" in Hebrew was the same phrase used of the Angel of Yahweh, Yahweh himself (Joshua 5:14)

Yahweh, God of hosts.[35] This Prince of the host of heaven is the Angel of Yahweh (Joshua 5:14-15), who is ultimately Jesus pre-incarnate (Revelation 9:11-16), our high priest (Hebrews 4:14).

The "host" of this Prince is defined by Daniel as "host of heaven," including the stars (8:10). I have described in detail elsewhere that "host of heaven" in the Bible is not merely a reference to the physical sun, moon, and stars but also to angelic Sons of God (Job 38:7), other angels (Psalms 148:2-3), and gods of the nations (Deuteronomy 4:12-20).[36]

This leads to the most natural conclusion that this symbolic prophecy of stars "being thrown to the ground and trampled" is fulfilled in heavenly powers being overthrown along with their earthly counterparts. This is the conflict of gods over nations. When the pagan ruler Antiochus captured the temple and profaned it, some of Yahweh's heavenly host were "given over to it together with the regular burnt offering because of the transgression" (Daniel 8:12). The heavenly conflict was tied to the earthly conflict. Because Israel had transgressed against Yahweh in her unfaithfulness, this empowered the pagan earthly and heavenly rulers to maintain temporary power over the holy temple of Yahweh. On earth as it is in heaven (Matthew 6:10b).

When Daniel hears a "holy one" speaking to another "holy one," some think that "holy one" is a reference to Israelites, or "saints" as it is sometimes translated. But "holy one" is tricky because it is used of both human Israelites[37] and heavenly divine beings around God's throne as well as Yahweh himself.[38] So context would dictate the meaning. The context of Daniel contains both. But when it comes to visions in Daniel, the holy ones are described explicitly as heavenly beings.

---

35 Psalm 59:5; 89:8; Isaiah 10:24, 33; Jeremiah 5:14; 15:16; 38:17; Amos 4:13; 5:27.

36 See also Deuteronomy 32:8-9, 17, 43. For detailed investigation of stars as divine see Brian Godawa *When Watchers Ruled the Nations: Pagan Gods at War with Israel's God and the Spiritual World of the Bible* (Texas: Warrior Poet Publishing, 2021), 27-37.

37 Daniel 7:18, 21-22; 25, 27; 8:24; Psalm 34:9; 16:3; 30:4.

38 Psalm 89:5, 7; Deuteronomy 33:2; Zechariah 14:5; Jude 14; Job 15:15.

For example in Daniel 4, the prophet sees a vision where he defines "a watcher, **a holy one**, came down from heaven" (4:13). Those Watchers make decrees, "decisions by the word of the **holy ones**" (4:17). And let us not forget that in Daniel 8, the original passage we are looking at, Daniel is also having a vision of these holy ones who are "host of heaven," not of earth.

So the context of Daniel 8 is very clearly a story of the earthly Antiochus trampling God's temple and people underfoot but with the simultaneous spiritual reality of the heavenly host over Israel being temporarily overcome.

The "transgression that makes desolate" is therefore a reference to the sin of Israel that brought on the abomination of desolation, i.e., the imposition of Zeus worship with its altars and pagan ritual behaviors coupled with the spiritual power that comes with such earthly victory.

But of course, Yahweh's will is never ultimately thwarted. Ultimately, both the power and defeat of Antiochus as well as the spiritual powers behind him are by the hand of Yahweh (Daniel 8:24-25). As king Nebuchadnezzar would ultimately learn:

> Daniel 4:35
> [Yahweh] does according to his will among the host of
>   heaven
>   and among the inhabitants of the earth;
> and none can stay his hand
>   or say to him, "What have you done?"

Partial or Dual Fulfillment?

At this point, some Bible prophecy speculators will concede that the little horn and abomination of desolation in Daniel 8 and 11 are fulfilled in Antiochus Epiphanes in 168-165 BC. But they argue that he is only a "partial fulfillment" of this prophecy. That there is still an abomination of desolation in our future which will also fulfill these prophecies in an ultimate sense. Put another way, they believe there is a short-term fulfillment in Antiochus and a long-term fulfillment in another ruler yet to come. Antiochus then becomes only a type of fulfillment but not the final one. He is either a "partial fulfillment" or one of dual or multiple fulfillments of the same prophecy. These speculators believe the prophecies are *really* pointing toward someone else in our future. Sometimes they will even argue that there are many "abominations of desolation" and "little horns" in history (Hitler, Mussolini, Stalin, etc.) that point toward this ultimate abomination of desolation.

This is a dangerous unbiblical hermeneutic.

Those who hold this view have not thought through what they are really arguing for. Their view ultimately reduces Bible prophecy to subjective arbitrary putty that can be pressed into any shape according to the personal subjective tastes of the interpreter. The result is that Bible prophecy can mean whatever any interpreter can make it fit. Let's look at how this plays out.

First, what does "partial fulfillment" even mean? Does that mean Antiochus only fulfilled some of the prophecies but not all of them? That would be empirically false. I have shown how that little horn Seleucid king and his abominable idol fulfilled *all the prophecies* related to the abomination of desolation in Daniel 8 and 11. To say that he only partially fulfilled those prophecies is to deny the biblical facts.

If by "partial" the interpreter means that it is only one of two or more fulfillments of the same prophecy, then they still have the problem of imposing their preconceived bias upon the text. Where in the Bible does it say these prophecies are about anything other than the singular historic events they predict? Nowhere. It either fulfills the prophecy or it does not. If it fulfills the prophecy, where does the prophet say there will be others? To see the historic fulfillment of these prophesies and declare two or more fulfillments of one prophecy is to claim a mystical or secret knowledge of the "real meaning" of the prophecy that is not apparent in the text. This would reduce prophecy to the arbitrary whim of every private interpretation.

Another problem with partial, dual, or multiple fulfillments is that Daniel's prophecies are specifically rooted in historical events that explicitly point to one time period of history that ended in Messiah in the first century. Consider the fact that Daniel's dream interpretation in Daniel 2 is all about the arrival of Messiah, who brings the Kingdom of God "in the days of these kings" (2:44). What kings? Daniel explains that Nebuchadnezzar's dream of the metallic statue symbolically represented four kingdoms in succession—the Babylonians, the Medo-Persians, the Greeks, and the Romans (2:36-43). These are exactly the kingdoms that we see in past history.

Daniel then says that the Messiah would bring his kingdom in the days of the last kingdom, that of Rome (2:34, 44-45). From that day forward, the Messiah's kingdom would grow to overcome all the other kingdoms (2:44-45). This all happened in history just as Daniel predicted. The Babylonians were conquered by the Medo-Persians, who were then conquered by the Macedonian Greek kingdom of Alexander the Great, whose kingdom was eventually overtaken by ancient Rome.

Some futurists try to deny the contiguous history in the prophecy, claiming that it is not about the first coming of Jesus but his second coming. They believe that the Roman kingdom of iron mixed with clay is not the ancient Roman kingdom into which Jesus came but that Daniel skips right over the coming of Messiah, jumping thousands of years later to his second coming. The Roman empire in the prophecy then becomes a "rebuilt Roman empire" in our future, not the ancient Roman empire that came right after the Greek empire in actual history.

This makes no sense and doesn't fit the prophecy. Why would Daniel, whose entire purpose is to predict the coming of Messiah after all these Gentile kingdoms, just ignore that first coming and jump thousands of years later to a second coming? It would turn the first coming into an inconsequential event.

There is nowhere in the text that says there is a gap of thousands of years before the last kingdom. On the contrary, they are successive kingdoms which happen to match history perfectly. Ancient Rome came after ancient Greece just as Nebuchadnezzar's dream predicted. Messiah came during that kingdom and brought it all down just a few centuries after his arrival—just as the "rock cut without hands" in the prophecy struck the statue at the Roman feet, demolishing it.

The futurist prejudice is so blinding it will eliminate or downplay the prophecy of the first coming of Messiah to maintain its presumed scenario for the future. Such interpretation denies the obvious fulfillment and inserts a two-plus-thousand-year gap that is not in the text to push the last kingdom into the future. The futurist engages in revising the Bible itself to keep their eschatological system from collapsing into absurdity.

To reinforce the interpretation that Daniel is speaking of the four kingdoms of our past history, the rest of his book chronicles that history in more detail through various other visions. Daniel has another vision under the Babylonian king Belshazzar that zooms in on the Medo-Persian kingdom and then the Greek kingdom to come (Daniel 8). He depicts Alexander the Great as a mighty goat that overcomes a ram symbolizing Medo-Persia. This actually happened in history. Then in 8:9-14, Daniel explains Antiochus Epiphanes and his abomination of desolation coming out of that Greek kingdom as a little horn that we have exegeted earlier.

In Daniel 10, we read about the spiritual principality of Persia who will soon be battling the principality of Greece just as the Greek kingdom of Alexander the Great eventually took over Persia in history. Then in Daniel 11, we get a dizzying series of wars between the "kings of the north" and the "kings of the south," which refer to the Syrian Wars between the Greek Seleucids and Ptolemies after Alexander (see my chart at the end of this book about fulfillment of Daniel 11 in the lead-up to and including the Syrian Wars of the second century BC).

Antiochus Epiphanes appears in 11:20 as the final willful king of that series who brings his abomination of desolation.

After Antiochus comes the final king at the time of the end and the events of Daniel 12 that are during the days of ancient Rome. All this narrative requires more exegesis than this small booklet can offer.[39] But I think I have shown enough details to make it clear that the context of Daniel from beginning to end is all about the four Gentile kingdoms that would oppress Israel until Messiah came. And that's what biblical history is, a history of Israel, not the Gentile world.

Over and over again, the book of Daniel spells out prophetic and symbolic references to the Babylonians, the Medo-Persians, the Greeks (especially the Seleucids and Ptolemies), and then the Romans. The context of Daniel is so clearly about Israel's past history until Messiah that to say it is also symbolic of a future fulfillment is to engage in interpretive violence against the text. It is wrenching prophecies out of their full context in the book and arbitrarily applying them to some speculative future that only the interpreter can know.

This brings me to another problem with this futurist catastrophe of interpretation. Some will argue that there is precedent for dual fulfillment claims in Daniel by pointing to Messianic prophecies that seem to have a short-term fulfillment in the Old Testament and a long-term fulfillment in the New Testament in Jesus. For instance, they will claim that prophecies like Isaiah 7 about the virgin birth of Messiah apply to a local referent. God is speaking to king Ahaz and telling him that a young maiden in his presence would have a child who would not be fully grown before King Rezin of Damascus and "the son of Remaliah" of Israel would find their land deserted.[40] New Testament

---

[39] For more details on Daniel's prophecies of history see my podcast series, "Daniel and End Times Prophecy": https://www.youtube.com/playlist?list=PL5TyMLcYh4AOPA4WGoSAr9rSxUEMgv2hC

[40] Gene M. Tucker, "The Book of Isaiah 1–39," in *New Interpreter's Bible*, ed. Leander E. Keck, vol. 6 (Nashville: Abingdon Press, 1994–2004), 111.

writers then tell us that these prophecies also apply to Jesus as the Messiah (Matthew 1:22-23).

This kind of dual fulfillment in messianic prophecy is another subject too complex to address here. It is sometimes called typology. But for the sake of argument, I will assume it is true. That some Old Testament prophecies spoken of Jesus as Messiah may also have a local referent in Old Testament history. Here is the problem for the futurist. The ones who have made the claim of dual fulfillment of Messianic prophecies are New Testament apostles, who were the New Testament equivalent of the Old Testament prophets. They spoke for God, and their writings became Scripture. Jesus had actually invested them with his authority as his representatives (John 14:26), his ultimate authorities on earth (1 Corinthians 12:28).

For a Christian to look at the New Testament apostles and to conclude that we now have the same authority to claim dual fulfillments of prophecies *that the apostles did not claim* is to place ourselves and our subjective interpretations in the place of apostolic authority or prophets of God.[41] One would be saying, "I have new revelation from God that tells me that the prophecies of Daniel, though fulfilled in the past history of the four Gentile kingdoms, *also* have a future fulfillment to come." That claim by definition is "new revelation" because there is no dual fulfillment in the text according to Daniel. Such a claim is bringing a new interpretation that extends beyond what the prophecy actually predicts and fulfills. It is adding to the Word of God.

I don't know any Christian who would want to make such an explicit claim. But that is exactly what one is doing when one says, "I can do what the apostles did. I can declare dual fulfillments beyond the text." Only a bona fide prophet of God can claim to speak for God and therefore make such connections as that "out of Egypt I called my Son" is also about Jesus (Hosea 11:1; Matthew 2:15). We do not have the

---

[41] The New Testament spiritual gift of prophecy is not the same as Old Testament prophets. The apostles are.

right to do what the apostles and prophets of God did in exegeting dual fulfillments, if that is in fact what they did.

But the implications are far worse. If one claims prophecies have dual or multiple fulfillments, then every prophecy can be so interpreted. That would mean there could be another Son of David born in Bethlehem of a virgin who would take the sins of the world upon himself. Outrageous! Yes, but as soon as you say you cannot do that, you have put an arbitrary restriction that contradicts your original interpreting principle. You have said prophecies can have dual fulfillments, just not *those* prophecies. But where do you get that restriction? And where do you stop? It's arbitrary. If the standard is that prophecies can have dual fulfillments, that means messianic prophecies can too. And why not triple fulfillments? Or more?

Well, you may say, Jesus already came and died for our sins once and for all, so that can't happen again. Precisely. Once a prophecy is fulfilled, there is no "dual fulfillment" or you reduce it to subjective putty that is hostage to the whims of interpreters and makes us all prophets of God. If I can find any kind of similarity or connection between arbitrary words in the Old Testament and something in today's world, I have claimed a new revelation of God's Word.

This is not so absurd or unrealistic as it sounds. There are religious "Christian" writers and speakers right now who interpret the Bible this way, taking Scriptures out of context and finding mystical new fulfillments in our day. I have read one of them claim that historical events of the Old Testament such as the story of Jezebel and Elijah are prophecy "templates" for events being fulfilled in our day in America. With the wave of an interpretive wand, the historical Old Testament account has been turned into prophecies for today without any justification from Scripture whatsoever. Not analogies, actual prophecies. And this man claims it is revelation from the Holy Spirit.

By that claim, his writing of these so-called prophecies should be considered Scripture. He probably wouldn't claim that, but it is the logical conclusion of his premises. If God is giving him new revelation that some historical story in the Old Testament is now a prophecy, then he should logically conclude that his "revelation" is the Word of God and should be written down as scripture. This is an obvious blasphemy in claiming new revelation after apostolic authority has passed away. This is not some obscure preacher in a small church somewhere. This is a mega-bestselling "teacher," and untold hundreds of thousands of Christians are following his delusion of false prophecies.

I hope you can see how this concept of multiple fulfillments of prophecy becomes an arbitrary rule of Bible interpretation that results in every person appointing themselves a prophet of their own interpretation of out-of-context Scripture. If prophecy has multiple fulfillments, why can't I claim that Abraham Lincoln's emancipation of the slaves is a "partial fulfillment" of "proclaiming liberty to the captives" in Isaiah 6:1? Or that the lion with eagle wings in Daniel's vision about Babylon is a dual prophecy about America because the eagle is our national bird and we are like a powerful lion in the world. All analogies become prophecies. The possible interpretations are literally endless, reducing Bible prophecies into putty that can be shaped by a million interpretations, making a million prophets of God. In the dual or multiple fulfillment view, prophecy becomes meaningless words that can be applied to anything to which the interpreter can make a connection.

3

The Future Abomination of Desolation

Daniel 9:26–27
And the people of the prince who is to come shall destroy
the city and the sanctuary. Its end shall come with a flood,
and to the end there shall be war. **Desolations** are decreed.
And he shall make a strong covenant with many for one
week, and for half of the week he shall put an end to
sacrifice and offering. And on **the wing of abominations
shall come one who makes desolate,** until the decreed
end is poured out on the **desolate.**"

Daniel 12:11
And from the time that the regular burnt offering is taken
away and the **abomination that makes desolate** is set up,
there shall be 1,290 days.

Spoken of by Daniel

As we saw earlier, Antiochus IV Epiphanes fulfilled the prophecies
about the abomination of desolation in Daniel chapters 8 and 11. But
there are two other passages in Daniel that talk about a second
abomination of desolation to come long after Antiochus Epiphanes is
gone. This abomination appears as indicated above in chapters 9 and
12. This is not partial or dual fulfillment but a biblically defined second
abomination of desolation that is different from the first.

I do not have the space here to explore this topic exhaustively. It is
one of those prophecies that has a dozen different interpretations. I
recommend _The Seventy Weeks and the Great Tribulation_ by Philip
Mauro. Some Bible scholars suggest that the abomination of desolation

spoken of in Daniel 9 and 12 is the same being as in Daniel 8 and 11. But they cannot be the same for three big reasons I have previously stated. One, the first abomination by Antiochus was described as only a desecration of the temple (religious pollution) while the second abomination includes both the desolation *and* the destruction of that temple, as well as the city (9:26). That is a very big difference. Two, the period of desolation for the first abomination was 2,300 days, or evenings and mornings (Daniel 8:14), while the period of desolation for the second abomination would be 1,290 days (Daniel 12:11). Three, the first abomination was to occur long *before* "the time of the end" (Daniel 11:27, 35) while the second abomination was explicitly stated to occur *during* "the time of the end" (Daniel 11:40; 12:4, 9), at "the end of days" (Daniel 12:13). No matter how one interprets "the end," it is a definite time period that was to occur long after that first abomination of desolation.

The informed reader will naturally ask if this is the abomination that Jesus predicted.

> Matthew 24:15–20
> [Jesus:] "So when you see the **abomination of desolation** spoken of by the prophet Daniel, standing in the holy place (let the reader understand)

I believe it is. And I will address Jesus later. For now, I want to see where Daniel himself is pointing. Then we will look at how Jesus confirms that future monster.

So, who is this second abominable desolator to come? Let's take a closer look at Daniel 9.

The Seventy Weeks

Probably the most famous messianic prophecy in the Old Testament is Daniel's vision of the 70 Weeks. This is because it predicts the coming Messiah within a specific number of years from a specific historical event—the decree to restore and rebuild Jerusalem, most likely fulfilled in the decree of Artaxerxes I around 457 BC (Nehemiah 2:1). From 457 BC to AD 30 (the death of Jesus the Anointed One) is 487 years, the middle of the 70th week of years (Daniel 9:27).[1]

The English phrase "70 weeks" is a translation of the Hebrew "70 sevens" of years, or 490 years. That chronology would place Messiah in the very lifetime of Jesus.[2] This is why messianic expectation was so high in the first century. But it also places the arrival of Messiah right before the arrival of one who would set up an "abomination of desolation," going on to defile and destroy both Jerusalem and her holy temple. Just exactly how are these two things, the Anointed One and Abomination, related in time and space? And what do they have to do with the abomination of desolation in the days of the Maccabees as discussed earlier in this book? Let's take a closer look at the 70 Weeks prophecy.

Daniel 9:24–27
[24] Seventy weeks are decreed about your people and your holy city, to finish the transgression, to put an end to sin, and to atone for iniquity, to bring in everlasting righteousness, to seal both vision and prophet, and to anoint the most holy. [25] Know therefore and understand that from the going out of the word to restore and build Jerusalem to the coming of an anointed one, a prince, there shall be seven weeks. Then for sixty-two weeks it shall be built again with squares and moat, but in a troubled time. [26] And after the sixty-two weeks, an anointed one shall be cut off and shall have nothing. And the people of the prince who is to come shall destroy the city and the sanctuary. Its end shall come with a flood, and to the end

---

[1] It is important to note that our dates for these events are not set in stone. At best, we can only get close, but not exact, as much as some Christians would prefer. Jay Rogers, *The Prophecy of Daniel in Preterist Perspective: The Easy Parts and the Hard Parts* (Media House, 2021), 13.

[2] Another theory is that the decree to restore and rebuild Jerusalem was that of Cyrus the Great of Babylon in 538 BC, which would still place Messiah in the rough time period of Jesus. In this view, the prophecy does not claim scientific precision, but rather approximation, which is not unwarranted in prophetic interpretation.

there shall be war. Desolations are decreed. ²⁷ And he shall make a strong covenant with many for one week, and for half of the week he shall put an end to sacrifice and offering. And on the wing of abominations shall come one who makes desolate, until the decreed end is poured out on the desolate.

Let's take a closer look at the first part of this passage. Daniel's prophecy was given to Israel. Because Israel had been unfaithful to Yahweh, he had punished his people with exile in Babylon, the city from which Daniel was writing. When Daniel states that 70 weeks is decreed for God's holy people and city, he is referring to Jeremiah's prophecy that the exile would last for 70 years (Jeremiah 25:8-12). Daniel is now amplifying that the 70 years of judgment would be multiplied because of the multiplied wickedness of Israel (Daniel 9:2, 5-7). Though they would come back from exile in 70 years as promised (Ezra 1:1), their transgression would not be forgiven for 70 weeks of years. The Hebrew word for "weeks" is actually seven. So Daniel is saying that the prophecy will be fulfilled within 70 sevens of years, or 490 years. At the end of that time, the Anointed One, Messiah, would arrive to complete the punishment and bring in the New Covenant of forgiveness.

When Daniel wrote of "**finishing the transgression, to put an end to sin and atone for iniquity**" (9:24), he was writing about the sin of Israel. When Messiah came, he would put an end to sin and atone for Israel's transgression of continuing disobedience to Yahweh. This was fulfilled when the angel of the Lord told Mary to call her child Jesus, "for he will save his people from their sins" (Matthew 1:21). When Jesus cried out "It is finished" on the cross, he was putting an end to sin with his once-for-all sacrifice that atoned for iniquity and **brought in everlasting righteousness**, just as Daniel prophesied (Hebrews 9:12-14).

Jesus confirmed the promise, or "**sealed both vision and prophet**" (Daniel 9:24), in fulfilling the messianic promise to which all the prophets had looked forward (1 Peter 1:10-12). Jesus was the seal on the scroll of God's prophecies. And he was the "**anointed, most holy.**" The English translation that there was to be an "anointing of a most holy *place*" is not in the original language. In the Hebrew, it only says "anoint a most holy." Contextually, that would be Jesus. Since Jesus was the Anointed One, he was the most holy for only he could stand in the Holy of Holies of Yahweh's temple as our perfect sinless high priest.

The prophecy then returns to proclaim when this prophecy clock would begin. But this is sometimes translated in a confusing way that throws off interpretations. Does Messiah the prince come after the first seven weeks as the ESV translates or after 69 weeks (7+62)? The NASB95 cuts through that confusion with some clarity.

> Daniel 9:25 (NASB95)
> "So you are to know and discern *that* from the issuing of a decree to restore and rebuild Jerusalem until Messiah the Prince *there will be* seven weeks and sixty-two weeks; it will be built again, with plaza and moat, even in times of distress.

Consider reading the passage this way. There are three events coming—the decree about Jerusalem, its actual rebuilding, and the coming of Messiah. Those are three events within two different time periods. The first event, the decree, launches the first time period of 7 sevens, or 49 years. The city of Jerusalem was rebuilt in Nehemiah's day within 49 years after the decree during the "**times of distress**" or "**troubled times**" of Nehemiah 4:18. Then after the next 62 sevens of years, or about 483 years after the decree, the prophecy predicted the coming of Messiah. Messiah comes after 7+62 weeks of years, or 483 years.

After Messiah comes (i.e., after that 62nd week), he would be "**cut off and shall have nothing**" (Daniel 9:26). We see this fulfilled in

Jesus's words on the cross: "My God, my God, why have you forsaken me?" (Matthew 27:46, taken from Psalm 22:1). Sin cuts off spiritual relationship. "For our sake he made [Jesus] to be sin who knew no sin, so that in him we might become the righteousness of God" (2 Corinthians 5:21).

Messianic Context of Daniel 9:24-26	
Daniel Verse	**New Testament Fulfillment**
Finish the transgression.	Daniel 9:5-6, 10-11.
Put an end to sin.	Hebrews 9:26; 1:3.
Atone for iniquity.	Colossians 1:14; John 1:29; 1 John 2:2.
Bring in everlasting righteousness.	2 Corinthians 9:9; Daniel 7:14; Matthew 6:33; 1 Corinthians 1:30.
Seal both vision and prophet.	Luke 18:31; 24:44; 21:22; Matthew 5:17-18.
Anoint a most holy place.	Luke 4:17–21; Isaiah 61:1-2.
Temple rebuilt in troubled times.	Nehemiah 4:18.
Messiah cut off and have nothing.	Matthew 27:46 (Psalm 22:1); 2 Corinthians 5:21.

So, 69 of the 70 weeks are fulfilled up to the time of Messiah Jesus. But the text actually says that the Messiah is cut off "after" 69 weeks (7 + 62). So, his cutting off occurs sometime after his arrival at the start of the 70th week. Jesus started his ministry at age 30 around the years AD 27-29. That was the end of the 69th week and the beginning of the 70th week. And we know that about 3-1/2 years into his ministry, Jesus was crucified. Remember that 3-1/2 years because it is going to be important.

Next, we are told that a people of the "**prince to come**" shall destroy the city and sanctuary (Jerusalem and the temple). Some link this prince to the one who later "comes on the wing of abominations" (Daniel 9:27). I do not believe this to be the case because in the previous verse, the Messiah ("anointed one") is described as *the prince who is to come*. There are not two princes here. There is only one, and he is the Messiah prince.

Christians might react negatively to this by asking how it is possible that the Messiah would destroy Jerusalem and the temple. After all, it was the Romans who destroyed Jerusalem and the temple in AD 70. Therefore, they must be the people of the "prince to come" this passage is talking about. To many Bible readers, it may sound contradictory to call the invading Roman armies "the people of Messiah." But biblically speaking, this is exactly how God talks. Whenever God judges a city or a people, he sovereignly uses pagan armies to achieve his purposes, and he describes the event as God's own armies or servants bringing judgment. Indeed, the pagan armies are often described as God's own hand bringing judgment. They are in effect, God's people or instruments.[3]

When Israel first entered the Promised Land, Yahweh told them that if they would disobey him, he would "bring a [foreign] nation against you from far away, from the end of the earth, swooping down like the eagle" (Deuteronomy 28:49).

When God judged Israel in Isaiah's day, God stated that he was using the pagan nation of Assyria and her king as an axe in his own hand (Isaiah 10:5, 15-16), that it was God who sent the Assyrians against Israel (v 6).

When the first temple and Jerusalem were destroyed by the Babylonians in 586 BC, Yahweh described Nebuchadnezzar as "his servant" and the invading pagan armies as his tribes sent upon Israel (Jeremiah 25:8-9).

When Babylon was then overthrown by the Medes, Isaiah described it as Yahweh mustering and sending his own army host (the pagan Medes) to punish and make the land a desolation (Isaiah 13:1-5, 11).

---

[3] Interestingly, even if one interprets this "prince to come" as a king separate from Messiah whose people destroy the sanctuary and city, it still fits with my paradigm. For I will argue that the "prince" or king was Titus Vespasian, Roman Imperial ruler of the Roman armies.

So it is most consistent with Scripture to understand that Daniel is saying that the Messiah will be the one who destroys Jerusalem and her temple by sending a pagan army to do his work of judgment.

And that destruction of Jerusalem would happen *after* Messiah was cut off.

We know Jesus was cut off from the Father on the cross sometime around AD 29-32. So how long after the cross is the destruction of Jerusalem and the temple? Some Christian prophecy pundits impose a two-thousand-year gap here and say that the last seven years of the prophecy have been put on hold to be fulfilled in our future. This prince must be a future "Antichrist" who destroys a new temple that has been rebuilt after its destruction in AD 70.

This is problematic for a couple reasons. First, there is no reference in the text to a *second* rebuilt temple, only to the temple that was built after 49 years in the days of Nehemiah. The text says that this rebuilt temple will be destroyed *after* Messiah is cut off. Historically, this occurred a mere generation after Jesus Christ was cut off from the Father on the cross. There is only one destruction and one rebuilt temple in the text. So when futurists insert a belief in a *second* rebuilt temple and *second* destruction after the one that actually happened in history, they are adding to the Word of God, not exegeting it.

Do you see the pattern of adding gaps where there are none in the text and skipping over biblically significant events for imaginary ones? In Daniel 2, they skip over the prophecy of Christ's first coming and apply it to the second coming. Now, they skip over the actual prophesied destruction of the temple and apply it to a future destruction of a temple that the text never claims will be built.

There is also no indication in Daniel's prophecy of a time gap between any of the weeks of years as some futurists seek to impose. These prophecy speculators believe that everything in the first 69 or 69-1/2 weeks of years was fulfilled by the time period of Messiah Jesus. But depending on their interpretation, they believe that either the last 7 years of the prophecy or the last 3-1/2 years of the prophecy have yet to be fulfilled in our current future. They place a gap of over two thousand years into the prophecy to maintain it is not yet entirely fulfilled, therefore we are still waiting for the last 7 or last 3-1/2 years to happen.

The big problem with this gap theory is that the seventy sevens of years are described as occurring continuously *without a gap*. There is not even the slightest hint of a gap of thousands of years between any of the continuous 70 weeks of years. Inserting a gap of two thousand years reveals a preconceived system that imposes an external artificial construct which does not exist in the actual biblical text.

So what did happen to that last 7-year part of the prophecy after Messiah? The answer can be found in the very next verse. In Daniel 9:27, we read that "*he* **shall make a covenant with many for one week, and for half of the week, he shall put an end to sacrifice and offering.**" Many futurists interpret this "he" to be a so-called Antichrist and that the last week of years is a seven-year tribulation in the distant future. In their speculative paradigm, this Antichrist supposedly makes a treaty with Israel that he breaks after three-and-a-half years. Then he puts an end to sacrifices in a rebuilt temple in Jerusalem.

But the grammar of the Daniel text does not support this interpretation. In fact, the "he" referred to in verse 27 is grammatically a reference to the prior **Messiah prince**. "He," the prince in this passage who makes a covenant and puts an end to sacrifice, is the Christ, NOT the Antichrist. It is literally the opposite of what many prophecy speculators suggest. As scholar Kenneth Gentry has written:

> The indefinite pronoun "he" … refers back to the last
> dominant individual mentioned: "Messiah" (v. 26a). The
> Messiah is the leading figure in the whole prophecy, so
> that even the destruction of the Temple is related to His

death. In fact, the people who destroy the Temple are providentially "His armies" (Matthew 22:2-7).[4]

Let's reread the prophecy and that seventieth week with this clarity.

Daniel 9:27
And he [Messiah] shall make a strong [new] covenant with many [remnant believers] for one week [7 years], and for half of the week [3 1/2 years] he [Messiah] shall put an end to sacrifice and offering [the cross ends sacrifice and offering].

So we see that the initiation of the new covenant kingdom begins with Christ's ministry (Matthew 4:17). The "half-week" of years is not in the middle of some 7-year tribulation future to us. It represents the approximate 3-1/2 years of Christ's ministry. Jesus was crucified and therefore cut off from the Father 3-1/2 years into that 70th week of years. That is the creation of the new covenant.

In the Bible, Satan does not make covenants with God's people. God does. The "strong covenant" cannot therefore be of an Antichrist. It is the new covenant of the Christ. The earlier verse in Daniel 9 already stated it was Messiah who would "**put an end to sin and atone for iniquity**" (9:24), not some future Antichrist. It was Jesus Christ's sacrifice that put an end to sacrifices and offerings once and for all (Hebrews 10:12).

It is also important to note that while the abomination of desolation in both the past and future versions in Daniel "takes away the daily burnt offering" (Daniel 11:31, 12:11), the text says that what Messiah the Prince does is different. With his once-for-all sacrifice on the cross, Messiah "puts an end to sin and atones for iniquity" (Daniel 9:24) and "puts an end to sacrifice and offering" (Daniel 9:27). The Abomination

---

4 Dr. Kenneth L. Gentry, Jr., "Daniel's Seventy Weeks," (Covenant Media Foundation).
http://www.cmfnow.com/articles/pt551.htm

forcibly defies the covenant. The Anointed One fulfills and brings the covenant to an end.

So if Jesus put an end to sacrifice at the cross 3-1/2 years into the final 70th week of prophecy, what happens in the last 3-1/2 years of that last week of years? Nothing needs to happen. The break in the middle of the last week is a prophetic sign of the brokenness of Messiah at that point. That perfect last seven is broken in the middle by the cross. But because of that break in the 70th week, within the next three and a half years, the gospel was spreading all over the world to the Gentiles.

Now for the last verse of the passage. This is where the abomination is finally noted. And this is finally a different individual than the Messiah prince. This one is called "the one who makes desolate."

> Daniel 9:27
> And on the wing of **abominations** shall come **one who makes desolate**, until the decreed end is poured out on the **desolate**.

As we noted earlier, this is not the exact term "abomination of desolation," but it is a confluence of those exact terms in synonymous parallel. And this desolation is tied back to the previous verse 26 that describes the destruction of the city and sanctuary. "Its end shall come with a flood, and to the end there shall be war. Desolations are decreed." Can you see how the two things are connected? Messiah ends old covenant sacrifice with the cross, then the city and temple of old covenant sacrifices are destroyed by an abominable one shortly afterward. In fact, within a generation.

So who is this abominable "one who makes desolate"?

Titus Vespasian

I will argue that the Roman general Titus Caesar Vespasianus is the bringer of the second abomination of desolation spoken of in Daniel 9 and 12. This occurred at the city of Jerusalem in the time period of AD 66-70. Let me set the historical stage for this fulfillment. In his Olivet discourse of Matthew 24, Jesus prophesied the destruction of the temple in Jerusalem of his day as God's judgment for their rejection of Messiah.

> Matthew 23:37-24:2
> "O Jerusalem, Jerusalem, the city that kills the prophets
> and stones those who are sent to it! How often would I
> have gathered your children together as a hen gathers her
> brood under her wings, and you were not willing! See,
> your house [holy temple] is left to you desolate...."
> Jesus left the temple and was going away, when his
> disciples came to point out to him the buildings of the
> temple. But he answered them, "You see all these, do you
> not? Truly, I say to you, there will not be left here one
> stone upon another that will not be thrown down."

Within 40 years of Jesus's prediction, the temple was destroyed just as he had predicted. This resulted from a Jewish revolt in Judea, then a province of Roman rule, around AD 66. The political, religious, and historical details of this series of events has fortunately been left to us in the writings of a Jewish historian named Flavius Josephus. His book *The Wars of the Jews* chronicles the narrative from before the revolt in AD 66 all the way up to the final destruction of the city of Jerusalem and its temple in AD 70.

At the time of the Jewish revolt, Nero was still Caesar of Rome, and he had been persecuting the Christians. This was the wicked king under whose reign the apostles like Peter and Paul were martyred. It was a major spiritual turning point in history for both Judaism and Christianity. In AD 67, Nero had sent his general Vespasian to quench the Jewish revolt. But when Nero died in 68, Vespasian came back to Rome to become the next Caesar. He sent his son Titus to finish the job in his stead.

Titus was a competent military general, but the revolt was widespread and took 3-1/2 years to put down (does that 3-1/2 number sound prophetically familiar?). He was described by Roman historian Suetonius as "the darling of the human race," a "highly educated Roman noble with diplomatic skill that served to conceal both his efficiency and his ruthlessness."[5] As a family representative of Vespasian, Titus was considered to carry the authority of Caesar. He was even called Caesar during the war.[6]

Titus first swept through Judea, subduing most of the Jewish cities before ending up in AD 69 at Jerusalem, where he besieged the city for 5 months before conquering it and entering the holy city and temple.

A story of Titus from the Talmud illustrates his blasphemous, abominable nature. It is written that Titus had entered the temple, now empty of its treasures, and demanded, "Where is their God, the rock in whom they trusted?" He then "blasphemed and raged against Heaven.… He took a whore by her hand, and went into the house of the Holy of Holies; he spread out a scroll of the Torah, and on it he f****d her."[7]

Josephus explains that the Romans brought their standards into the temple, "and there did they offer sacrifices to them, and there did they make Titus imperator, with the greatest acclamations of joy."[8] Roman standards included an image of Caesar as god. They were a pagan abomination that signaled God's desolating absence from the temple.[9]

Josephus then claims that Titus plundered the temple of its treasures and ordered all the surviving priests to be put to death to perish along with the temple.[10] According to Josephus, the temple was burnt

---

[5] Brian W. Jones, "Titus (Emperor)," ed. David Noel Freedman, *The Anchor Yale Bible Dictionary* (New York: Doubleday, 1992), 581.

[6] Dio Cassius, *Histories* 65.1.1-4: "Vespasian was declared emperor by the senate also, and Titus and Domitian were given the title of Caesars. The consular office was assumed by Vespasian and Titus while the former was in Egypt and the latter in Palestine."

[7] *Babylonian Talmud Gittin* 5:6, I.12.A–D. Jacob Neusner, *The Babylonian Talmud: A Translation and Commentary, vol. 11b* (Peabody, MA: Hendrickson Publishers, 2011), 243–244.

[8] Flavius Josephus, *The Wars of the Jews* 6.6.1, §316.

[9] Flavius Josephus, *The Wars of the Jews* 2.9.2 §169-170.

[10] Flavius Josephus, *The Wars of the Jews* 6.6.1, §316, 321

on the same exact day, the 10th day of the month Ab, "upon which [the first temple] was formerly burnt by the king of Babylon."

The historian concludes that in the Roman war with the Jews, 1,100,00 Jews perished and 97,000 were taken into slavery. He concludes with hyperbolic words that echo Jesus: "Accordingly the multitude of those that therein perished exceeded all the destructions that either men or God ever brought upon the world."[11]

Of this city and sanctuary destruction, Daniel 9:26 says, "Its end shall come with a flood, and to the end there shall be war." The use of "flood" here is not a literal tsunami of water but a metaphoric description of the overwhelming speed and unstoppable force of God's judgment, a common image in Old Testament prophecy (Isaiah 28:17; Jeremiah 47:2). But there's even more to it than that. The use of flood language evokes Noah's flood, which was theologically communicated in Genesis as being a symbolic return to the chaos of pre-creation in order for God to start over with the creation of a new covenant with Noah. Biblically speaking, the destruction of the Jerusalem temple was symbolic of God reducing the old covenant system as embodied in that temple into chaos so he could establish his "new creation," the new covenant through Christ (2 Corinthians 5:17).[12]

So Titus would perfectly fit Daniel's prophetic portrayal of the "one who comes on the wing of abominations and makes desolate" by destroying both city and temple and bringing abomination and desolation to that sacred space. What's more, the desolation/destruction took place after Messiah made his new covenant just 40 years earlier—just as Daniel's prophecy stated. The Jerusalem temple was the incarnation of the old covenant. So once the new covenant was

---

[11] Flavius Josephus, *The Wars of the Jews* 6.9.3-4, §420, 429.

[12] For more detail on the temple and the New Covenant, see, Brian Godawa, Israel in Bible Prophecy: The New Testament Fulfillment of the Promise to Abraham (Warrior Poet Publishing, 2021), 47-53. Interestingly, the first temple being destroyed by the Babylonians in 586 BC was also described by the prophets Isaiah and Jeremiah as a decreation return to chaos: Isaiah 24:1-23; Jeremiah 4:23-26.

established, the old covenant symbol, the temple, was destroyed by God through the abominable pagan leader Titus (Hebrews 8:13; 9:8-9).

But we are not done with the abomination of desolation. There is one last passage in Daniel 12:11 that mentions it again. And again, the entire chapter has often been interpreted as yet-to-take-place in our future. And yet again, I would argue for a first century fulfillment of the second abomination of desolation under the actions of Titus Vespasian, the "one who makes desolate."

Let's run through the passage verse by verse.

Daniel 12

> Daniel 12:11–13
> [11] And from the time that the regular burnt offering is taken away and the **abomination that makes desolate** is set up, there shall be 1,290 days. [12] Blessed is he who waits and arrives at the 1,335 days. [13] But go your way till the end. And you shall rest and shall stand in your allotted place at the end of the days."

Daniel 12 is the final section of the prophecies of Daniel. This section actually begins at Daniel 11:36 with the final "willful king" at the time of the end. Remember, chapter separations are not in the original text. So when Daniel 12:1 begins by saying, "At that time shall arise Michael," he is referring to the "time of the end" that he was just addressing a few verses earlier in 11:35, 40. It is one continuous flow of history.

So when exactly is this "time of the end"? Many Bible prophecy speculators assume it is the end of history when Jesus returns. But they would be seriously wrong. I do not have the space here to exegete every detail of this section, so I will stick to a few major points that argue against the context of our future and for the context of our past in the first-century days of ancient Rome and Titus Vespasian (if the reader wants more detail, see my podcast series, Daniel and End Times

<u>Prophecy</u>).[13] Please keep in mind I am not arguing here that there is no return of Christ in our future but simply arguing that Daniel is not talking about that event. He is talking about the first coming of Messiah at the end of the Gentile kingdoms.

The final kingdom of Daniel's four kingdoms. First, remember the context of Daniel's prophecies that we established earlier on. Daniel's prophecies are all about the four kingdoms that would rule over Israel until Messiah came: Babylon, Medo-Persia, Greece, and Rome. The vision of the large statue of four metals (Daniel 2), then the vision of the four great hybrid beasts from the sea (Daniel 7), and then the vision of the charging ram and the one-horned goat (Daniel 8) all reiterate those four kingdoms with differing focus. We read about Babylon in Daniel 1-7, then Medo-Persia in Daniel 8-11, which occurred during the lifetime of Daniel. Daniel 11-12 follows with predictions about the final two kingdoms of Greece and Rome. Messiah would come "in the days of these kings," specifically Rome, to usher in Messiah's new covenant kingdom (Daniel 2:44-45; 9:24-27).

Remember we have already seen that Daniel 11 chronicles with amazing precision the third kingdom, Greece, with its Syrian Wars of the third century BC, ending with the abomination of desolation by King Antiochus IV Epiphanes (11:21-35). So when Daniel begins to address the final king that "shall do as he wills" at "the time of the end" in 11:36-45, we are in the fourth and final kingdom of Rome. After all, what kingdom comes immediately after Greece in Daniel's prophetic timeline? Not some future symbolic or speculative rebuilt Roman kingdom thousands of years later but the real-world Rome that arose after Greece in real-world history. The big picture context of Daniel demands that the time of the end is during the ancient Roman kingdom (empire).

But isn't the time of the end the end of all time?

---

[13] https://www.youtube.com/playlist?list=PL5TyMLcYh4AOPA4WGoSAr9rSxUEMgv2hC

57

Time of the end. In Daniel 12, the divine messenger explains that the second abomination of desolation comes at the time of the end or the end of the days.

> Daniel 12:9, 13
> He said, "Go your way, Daniel, for the words are shut up and sealed until **the time of the end**.… But go your way **till the end**. And you shall rest and shall stand in your allotted place at **the end of the days**."

When they read those words, too many Christians impose their own preconceived cultural assumptions upon the phrases "time of the end," "end of the days," or "till the end." They read them out of context. The primary rule of understanding the Bible in its ancient context is to let Scripture interpret Scripture. When we read the words "time of the end," we must not *assume* it means what we want it to mean, the end of all time or the end of the space-time universe. We must ask according to biblical precedent and context, "The end of what?" Let's let Daniel tell us exactly what he means by the end.

> Daniel 8:19–23
> [19] He said, "Behold, I will make known to you what shall be at **the latter end of the indignation ["curse"]**, for it refers to the appointed **time of the end**. [20] As for the ram that you saw with the two horns, these are the kings of Media and Persia. [21] And the goat is the king of Greece. And the great horn between his eyes is the first king. [22] As for the horn that was broken, in place of which four others arose, four kingdoms shall arise from his nation, but not with his power. [23] And at **the latter end of their kingdom, when the transgressors have reached their limit,** a king of bold face, one who understands riddles, shall arise.

The time of the end is the "latter end of the indignation" or curse upon Israel when the transgressors have reached their limit. This occurs at the latter end of the four Greek "horn" kingdoms that came out of the horn of Alexander. Antiochus Epiphanes was at that latter end of those Greek kingdoms. In fact, it was during his reign that the Roman republic asserted her power over the Greek kingdoms of Seleucia and Ptolemies of Egypt. After the death of Antiochus Epiphanes, those Greek kingdoms began to crumble under Rome's ascendancy. Shortly thereafter in 65 BC under Julius Caesar, Rome would evolve into the Roman empire, the last of Daniel's four kingdoms.

Daniel 9:24-27 states that Messiah would finish the transgression of Israel, put an end to sin, atone for iniquity, and bring in his everlasting kingdom of righteousness. Israel's curse would be ended with the coming of Messiah. In context, Daniel was writing about the Messiah *ending* the transgression of Israel and *ending* sin with his atonement for iniquity at the cross (Daniel 9:24). And that was linked to *the end* of the holy city and temple (9:26). Daniel reiterates this *end* of the temple again in 12:11 with the second abomination of desolation. So "the end" in Daniel's prophecy is not the end of history or the end of time. It is the end of Israel's sin of idolatry against Yahweh through Messiah that would occur in the days of Rome at the end of the four kingdoms.

11:36-45 – the final "king that shall do as he wills … at the time of the end" is a ruler who is a part of that fourth and final kingdom. There are several strong options for who this Roman king was: Julius Caesar and the line of Caesars, the Roman general Titus, or King Herod the Great. I am not certain as to which of these three positions I am most persuaded. I find them each compelling. I would recommend further study.[14] But I lean toward King Herod, the Edomite king over Judea and

---

[14] Jay Rogers argues that it is the line of Caesars beginning with Julius: Jay Rogers, *In the Days of These Kings: The Book of Daniel in Preterist Perspective* (Clermont, FL: Media House International, 2017).
Duncan McKenzie makes a good argument that Titus is the king of Daniel 11:36: McKenzie PhD, Duncan W., *The Antichrist and the Second Coming: A Preterist Examination Volume I* (Kindle Locations 2896-2903). Xulon Press.
Philip Mauro argues for Herod the Great: Philip Mauro, *The Seventy Weeks and the Great Tribulation: A Study of the Last Two Visions of Daniel, and of the Olivet Discourse of the Lord Jesus Christ* (Public Domain, 1921, 1944),

client king of Rome. He certainly magnified himself above gods (Daniel 11:36). He was king when Messiah was born to end "the indignation" of Israel (11:36). As an Edomite, he paid no attention to the god of his fathers, Abraham, Isaac, and Jacob (11:37). He built mighty fortresses as he rejected Yahweh (11:38-39). He divided his land for favors (11:39). The final section of this king's interaction with the kings of the south and north (11:40-45) reflects Herod's experience with Caesar Augustus (king of the north) and Egyptian queen Cleopatra (king of the south). The major actor "he" in that section is the king of the north, Augustus. The passage describes his victory over Antony and Cleopatra in the battle of Actium in 31 BC.[15]

As Bible commentator James Jordan explains:

> Why is attention given to these events, out of the many in Herod's reign? I believe it is because these events (a) fully established Rome's domination over the near east once and for all; (b) ended the separate history of the South, thus bringing to an end the Alexandrian history that began in Daniel 11:3; and (c) established Octavian Caesar, soon to take the name Augustus, as ruler of the Roman empire, thus setting the stage for the events described when Daniel's sealed book is reopened in the book of Revelation [in the first century].[16]

12:1-3 – "And many of those who sleep in the dust of the earth shall awake, some to everlasting life, and some to shame and everlasting contempt." This is a famous passage that many assume refers to the

---

James Jordan also makes a persuasive case that the "Little Horn" of Daniel 8:9-26 is also Herod the Great, rather than Antiochus Epiphanes. This would not change the overall interpretation or the other passages that still refer to Antiochus. See James B. Jordan, *The Handwriting on the Wall: A Commentary on the Book of Daniel* (Powder Springs, GA: American Vision, 2007), 424-437.

[15] For a good narrative of this fulfillment see, Bruce Gore, *Historical and Chronological Context of the Bible* (Bruce Gore, 2006), Chapter 11, pages 15-16.

[16] James B. Jordan, *The Handwriting on the Wall: A Commentary on the Book of Daniel* (Powder Springs, GA: American Vision, 2007), 606–607.

physical resurrection at the end of history and the return of Christ. But since it takes place in the days of ancient Rome, it is not in fact about the second coming. It is about the *first coming* of Christ. It wouldn't make sense for Daniel to completely skip over the most important hope of the Old Testament, the first coming of Messiah, to talk about a second coming out of context. This resurrection is simply Daniel's reiteration of his contemporary Ezekiel's obvious metaphorical resurrection of Israel when Messiah comes (Ezekiel 37). Many Jews would rise from their spiritual death to everlasting life in Christ (through faith) while some of those Jews would spiritually rise to shame in rejecting Jesus and end in everlasting contempt. Jesus would be the spiritual Promised Land of Israel unto which they would be regathered (Hebrews 9:15; 11:8-16; 12:22-24).[17]

12:7 – "[the length of time for these predictions to take place] would be for a time, times, and half a time…"

A time, times, and half a time is another way of saying 3 1/2. "Titus's campaign of destruction against the Jews lasted exactly three-and-a-half years (March/April AD 67 to August/September AD 70) and resulted in the destruction of the Jewish nation."[18]

12:7 – "…and that when the shattering of the power of the holy people comes to an end all these things would be finished."

The "power of the holy people" in the Bible is the covenant. The shattering of that power or covenant was the end of the old covenant that was historically and publicly ended in AD 70 with the destruction of the incarnation of that old covenant system, the holy temple (Matthew 21:38-44, fulfilling Joshua 23:16; Galatians 4:24-31).

---

[17] For a detailed explanation of how Jesus Christ fulfills the Land Promise see my book, Brian Godawa, Israel in Bible Prophecy: The New Testament Fulfillment of the Promise to Abraham (Warrior Poet Publishing, 2021), 22-32.
[18] McKenzie PhD, Duncan W., *The Antichrist and the Second Coming: A Preterist Examination Volume I* (Xulon Press. Kindle Edition).

12:9 – "He said, "Go your way, Daniel, for the words are shut up and sealed until the time of the end."
12:13 – "But go your way till the end. And you shall rest and shall stand in your allotted place at the end of the days."

The "time of the end" is not "the end of time." "End of the days" does not mean "end of all days" but merely the end of the days for these prophecies of the four Gentile kingdoms (12:12). Those days were ended with the AD 70 destruction of the temple in Jerusalem.

12:11-12 – "And from the time that the regular burnt offering is taken away and the abomination that makes desolate is set up, there shall be 1,290 days. Blessed is he who waits and arrives at the 1,335 days."

The Hebrew grammar underlying this verse is unclear as to whether the taking away of the burnt offering is first, the arrival of the abomination of desolation is first, or whether the two incidents are to be considered together as the starting point for the days.

The ancient Jewish historian Josephus indicates the exact date in AD 70 when the daily sacrifices had stopped during the war with Rome.

> Josephus *Wars of the Jews*, 6.2.1 (93)
> And now Titus gave orders to his soldiers that were with him to dig up the foundations of the tower of Antonia, and make him a ready passage for his army to come [into the Jerusalem temple] … on that very day, which was the seventeenth day of Panemus [Tamuz], the sacrifice called "the Daily Sacrifice" had failed, and had not been offered to God.[19]

Based on this interpretation of the ending of the sacrifice in AD 70, Bible scholar Philip Mauro concluded:

---

[19] Flavius Josephus and William Whiston, *The Works of Josephus: Complete and Unabridged* (Peabody: Hendrickson, 1987), 731.

The first approach of the Roman armies under Cestius is described by Josephus in his book of Wars, II 17, 10. This was in the month corresponding to our November, A.D. 66. The taking away of the daily sacrifice was in the month Panemus, corresponding to the Hebrew Tammuz, and our July, A.D. 70. Thus the measure of time between the two events was three years, and part of a fourth [or 1,290 days].[20]

Those Roman armies that were previously under Cestius would return 3 1/2 years later led personally by the co-emperor Titus. When Titus captured the holy city and temple, it was the end of the siege but not the end of the war atrocities that would commence upon victory. The additional 45 days that resulted in Daniel's blessing to those surviving 1,335 days is a reference to those few Jews who had been able to hide or escape the pillage and plunder of the Roman forces in the city.

To conclude, let's look at the whole of the Daniel prophecy again with my notations to see how it all flows.

> Daniel 9:24–27 (NASB95)
> [24] Seventy weeks [of years or 490 years] have been decreed for your people [Israel] and your holy city [Jerusalem], to finish the transgression [of Israel's spiritual idolatry], to make an end of sin, to make atonement for iniquity [through the cross], to bring in everlasting righteousness [with the gospel], to seal up vision and prophecy [that have all been pointing to Jesus] and to anoint the most holy [Jesus].
> [25] "So you are to know and discern that from the issuing of a decree to restore and rebuild Jerusalem [by Artaxerxes in 457-8 BC] until Messiah the Prince [Jesus] there will be seven weeks [49 years] and sixty-two weeks [+434 years =

---

[20] Mauro, Philip. *The Seventy Weeks and the Great Tribulation* (K-Locations 2288-2319). K-Edition.

483 years]; it will be built again, with plaza and moat, even in times of distress [in the days of Nehemiah].
²⁶ Then after the sixty-two weeks [after 483 years around AD 30-32] the Messiah will be cut off [from the Father on the cross for us by taking on our sin] and have nothing, and the people [Roman soldiers] of the prince who is to come [Jesus as sovereign God using them] will destroy the city [Jerusalem] and the sanctuary [the temple]. And its end will come with a flood [in AD 70]; even to the end there will be war; desolations are determined [as Jesus predicted and Josephus described in *The Wars of the Jews*].
²⁷ And he [Messiah Jesus] will make a firm [new] covenant with the many [remnant believers] for one week [the beginning of the 70th week of years in AD 30], but in the middle of the week [3 1/2 years later in AD 33] he [Jesus] will put a stop to sacrifice and grain offering [by his once for all sacrifice on the cross]; and [within that generation, or 40 years] on the wing of abominations will come one [Titus the Roman general] who makes desolate [the temple], even until a complete destruction [in AD 70], one that is decreed, is poured out on the desolate.

Because of their preconceived eschatology, most futurists separate the abomination of desolation from the coming of Messiah. They think that the Seventy Weeks prophecy is talking about the first coming of Jesus, then jumps ahead thousands of years into the future to talk about an Antichrist who is the abomination of desolation. They have to impose an imagined third rebuilt temple and destruction and ignore the second rebuilt temple and destruction spoken of in the text. They have to stick a 2,000-year gap into the prophecy, which simply isn't there. It's not even hinted at. They must add to the Word of God to keep their system working. In reality, the context consistently fits the first century where all those things occurred.

And if you don't believe me, let's ask Jesus.

Jesus and the Abomination of Desolation

It is well known that Jesus spoke of the coming "abomination of desolation spoken of by the prophet Daniel" (Matthew 24:15). When futurist prophecy speculators read his statement that took place on the Mount of Olives, they see it as the Antichrist, the Beast, some demonic person in our own future who has yet to appear and set foot in the temple in Jerusalem (which is supposedly yet to be rebuilt). This is alleged to happen in the midst of a "great tribulation" in our future and heralds a betrayal of a treaty made between the Antichrist and Israel. Unfortunately, none of this imagined futuristic science fiction is in the passage, let alone in the entire Bible. Let's take a look at Jesus's words in biblical context.

> Matthew 24:15–20
> [Jesus:] "So when you see the **abomination of desolation** spoken of by the prophet Daniel, standing in the holy place (let the reader understand), [16] then let those who are in Judea flee to the mountains. [17] Let the one who is on the housetop not go down to take what is in his house, [18] and let the one who is in the field not turn back to take his cloak. [19] And alas for women who are pregnant and for those who are nursing infants in those days! [20] Pray that your flight may not be in winter or on a Sabbath.

This Generation

So many Christians come to this passage with a preconceived assumption that it is in our future when the actual context of the prophecy through Jesus's own words says it already happened in our past to his generation.

Jesus himself tells us the interpretive key to the abomination of desolation in several ways. First and most important is that the entire prophecy of events to happen in Matthew 24, including the abomination of desolation," is bookended by a repeated phrase: *this generation*.

Matthew 23:36
Truly, I say to you, all these things will come upon **this generation.**

Matthew 24:34
Truly, I say to you, **this generation** will not pass away until all these things take place.

So Jesus tells us that all these things he was predicting—the destruction of the temple, wars and rumors of wars, persecution, apostasy, the abomination of desolation—were to come upon his generation that was rejecting him. In fact, most of them would not pass away until it occurred (Matthew 16:28).

Like the 40-year wilderness generation that was judged for their unbelief, so Jesus's generation would be judged for their unbelief. Their rejection of Messiah is exactly what Jesus was explaining in Matthew 23.

Matthew 23:36–24:2
"Truly, I say to you, all these things will come upon **this generation**. O Jerusalem, Jerusalem, the city that kills the prophets and stones those who are sent to it! … See, **your house [the temple] is left to you desolate**." … Jesus left the temple and was going away, when his disciples came to point out to him the buildings of the temple. But he answered them, "You see all these, do you not? Truly, I say to you, **there will not be left here one stone upon another that will not be thrown down**."

A generation was about 40 years, another symbolic number. And it just so happens that the second temple was destroyed about 40 years later in AD 70 before Jesus's generation had passed away.

There have been attempts to try to spin away the plain meaning of the phrase "this generation" to mean anything other than the generation to whom Jesus was speaking. All of them fall flat in the face of the explicit definition given by Matthew and all the New Testament. Everywhere Matthew uses the phrase "this generation," it is a reference *to the contemporary generation of Jesus*, the ones to whom he was speaking. Not only that, but it was also most often used as a derogatory term of judgment upon those who were rejecting Jesus as Messiah.[21]

> Matthew 12:41
> The men of Nineveh will rise up at the judgment with **this generation** and condemn it, for they repented at the preaching of Jonah, and behold, something greater than Jonah is here.

> Luke 17:25
> But first he must suffer many things and be rejected by **this generation**.

> Luke 11:50–51
> So that the blood of all the prophets, shed from the foundation of the world, may be **charged against this generation**.... Yes, I tell you, it will be required of **this generation**.

So when Jesus predicts the destruction of the temple in Matthew 23:37-24:2 as judgment upon the first-century Jews for rejecting Messiah and states that everything included with that judgment would occur to "this generation," he is referencing his generation to whom he was speaking. When Jesus uses the personal second person accusative "you" over 35 times—"when *you* see," "when such and such happens to *you*"—directly to his audience, it is safe to say that he meant the generation to whom he was speaking, not some future generation of people.

Imagine being a person listening to Jesus telling you that when you see these things and when these things happen to you, then you should know that destruction is near. Then you discover that he wasn't talking to you at all but was speaking to and about a future generation of people

---

thousands of years from your generation. You could fairly accuse Jesus of misleading his entire audience. Of course, I do not believe Jesus would ever mislead or lie. My point is that the claim that Jesus was not speaking to his audience but to an imaginary future one is tantamount to such misinformation.

In my novel series Chronicles of the Apocalypse, I tell the story of the destruction of Jerusalem and the temple in AD 70 by the Roman forces of Titus. I based it on the only existing full manuscript detailing the infamous event by one of its own participants, Jewish historian Flavius Josephus. His narrative reads like a virtual point-by-point fulfillment of Jesus's prophecy in Matthew 24.

Here are a couple paragraphs from Josephus's account of the AD 70 destruction of Jerusalem and its temple where he claims fulfillment of Daniel's two abominations of desolation as referencing successively Antiochus Epiphanes and Rome under Titus. Josephus also considered the Romans as God's means of judgment. If Josephus wasn't a Jew who most definitely didn't accept Jesus as Messiah, you would think he was a Christian quoting Jesus.

> Flavius Josephus, *Antiquities* 10.276
> And indeed it so came to pass, that our nation suffered these things under Antiochus Epiphanes, according to Daniel's vision, and what he wrote many years before they came to pass. In the very same manner **Daniel also wrote concerning the Roman government, and that our country should be made desolate by them**.

> Flavius Josephus, *The Wars of the Jews* 6.2.1 §110
> And are not both the city and the entire temple now full of the dead bodies of your countrymen? It is God therefore, **it is God himself who is bringing on this fire, to purge that city and temple by means of the Roman**s, and is going to pluck up this city, which is full of your **pollutions**.

Flee to the Mountains

Another element of context to the abomination of desolation passage that reinforces a first-century fulfillment is the advice Jesus gives to his audience to flee Judea when they see the abomination of desolation at the gates.

> Matthew 24:17-20
> Then let those who are in Judea flee to the mountains. Let the one who is on the housetop not go down to take what is in his house, and let the one who is in the field not turn back to take his cloak. And alas for women who are pregnant and for those who are nursing infants in those days! Pray that your flight may not be in winter or on a Sabbath.

None of this could apply to the present-day thousands of years after Christ. Fleeing to the mountains today would be meaningless in the face of modern travel and war technology. Winter, Sabbath, and pregnancy would not be problematic for modern travelers. Back in the first century, the mountains surrounding Israel were actual places of refuge from the war that had spread throughout the land. But it would be difficult to flee there carrying small children, ferrying household goods in carts or wagons, or even just for the elderly, incapacitated, or heavily pregnant.

Jesus was telling his followers how to escape the judgment that was coming upon Jerusalem and Israel for rejecting Messiah. And escape they did. Early church historian Eusebius recorded how the Christians followed Jesus' warnings.

> Eusebius, *Ecclesiastical History* 3:5
> But the people of the church in Jerusalem had been commanded by a revelation, vouchsafed to approved men there before the war, to leave the city and to dwell in a certain town of Perea called Pella. And when those that believed in Christ had come thither from Jerusalem, then, as if the royal city of the Jews and the whole land of Judea

were entirely destitute of holy men, the judgment of God at length overtook those who had committed such outrages against Christ and his apostles, and totally destroyed that generation of impious men.[22]

My second book in the *Chronicles of the Apocalypse* series, Remnant: Rescue of the Elect tells this story in dramatic fiction. The Christians were spared from God's judgment because they were no longer part of the old system, the old age of the old covenant. They had both figuratively and literally fled all of it. God was destroying the temple as the incarnation of that old covenant.

Since most Jews did not embrace the new covenant, they were in a dead religion. The Roman army was like vultures gathering around the carcass of that dead religion to finish it off just as Jesus stated in this same Olivet discourse.

> Matthew 24:28
> Wherever the corpse is, there the vultures will gather.

But there is even more hermeneutical help that Jesus gives us in interpreting his words. More precisely, Luke gives us a literal explanation of what the "abomination of desolation" actually was in his generation.

Surrounded by Pagan Armies

Let's take a step back for more context. Matthew uses the Hebrew term abomination of desolation. This is important because the book of Matthew was written to Jews. It has many Hebraisms and Old Testament references and concepts that most Jews would know when reading them.

---

[22] Eusebius of Caesaria, "The Church History of Eusebius," in *Eusebius: Church History, Life of Constantine the Great, and Oration in Praise of Constantine*, ed. Philip Schaff and Henry Wace, trans. Arthur Cushman McGiffert, vol. 1, *A Select Library of the Nicene and Post-Nicene Fathers of the Christian Church, Second Series* (New York: Christian Literature Company, 1890), 138.

The gospel of Luke was written more for a Gentile audience, so he tended to explain things or translate them for the non-Hebrew. The abomination of desolation is one of those things Luke translated for us.

Luke 21 and Mark 13 both contain the same sermon also found in Matthew 24. But there are some variations in the text. Let me put them side by side so you can see the obvious correlation.

Matthew 24:15–16	Luke 21:20–22	Mark 13:14 (NASB95)
"So **when you see the abomination of desolation** spoken of by the prophet Daniel, standing in the holy place (let the reader understand), then let those who are in Judea flee to the mountains."	"But **when you see Jerusalem surrounded by armies**, then know that its desolation has come near … Then let those who are in Judea flee to the mountains."	"But **when you see the abomination of desolation standing where it should not be** (let the reader understand), then those who are in Judea must flee to the mountains."

The Hebrew image of "abomination of desolation" in Matthew and Mark is translated by Luke to be "Jerusalem surrounded by armies." So Luke makes clear that the correct interpretation intended by Jesus of "abomination of desolation" is *Jerusalem being surrounded by armies.* Specifically, pagan idolatrous armies.

Did this happen in the first century as we have been arguing? Why, yes, it did. In A.D. 66, the abominable Roman armies did in fact surround Jerusalem just as Jesus had foretold. In this sense, they were "standing in a holy place" around the holy city "where it [the pagan army] should not be." Like Antiochus Epiphanes and his Greek armies setting up their idol of Zeus, so a general of Titus named Cestius with his Roman legions surrounded Jerusalem with their idolatrous standards of Caesar, the abomination of desolation (images of desolation). Providentially, Josephus tells us that for some unknown reason, Cestius stopped short of attacking the temple and just left with all his army. This allowed the Christians of the city the opportunity to flee to the mountains.

A couple years later, Titus returned with that army and finished what was started by conquering the city of Jerusalem and capturing the temple. While there, he set up Rome's idolatrous standards of Caesar in the temple as an abomination of desolation. Jewish historian Josephus described the event.

> And now the Romans … upon burning of the holy house itself, and of all the buildings round about it, brought their ensigns to the temple … and there did they offer sacrifices to them, and there did they make Titus imperator, with the greatest acclamations of joy.[23]

It could not be more clear. Pagan rulers and their armies are abominable defilers of sacred space.

The destruction of the city and temple were a main focus of the prophetic near-future for Jesus and the apostles. In fact, Jesus referred on another occasion to the destruction of the city of Jerusalem as punishment for the Jews not recognizing the time of the visitation of God in Messiah.

> Luke 19:41–44
> And when he drew near and saw the city [Jerusalem], he wept over it, saying, "Would that you, even you, had known on this day the things that make for peace! But now they are hidden from your eyes. For the days will come upon you, when your enemies will set up a barricade around you and surround you and hem you in on every side and tear you down to the ground, you and your

---

[23] Flavius Josephus, *The Wars of the Jews* 6.6.1, §316. Josephus also describes the standards as considered idolatrous by the Jews in *The Wars of the Jews* 2.9.2 §169-170 "Now Pilate, who was sent as procurator into Judea by Tiberius, sent by night those images of Caesar that are called Ensigns, into Jerusalem. (170) This excited a very great tumult among the Jews when it was day; for those that were near them were astonished at the sight of them, as indications that their laws were trodden underfoot: for those laws do not permit any sort of image to be brought into the city." Flavius Josephus and William Whiston, *The Works of Josephus: Complete and Unabridged* (Peabody: Hendrickson, 1987), 608.

children within you. And they will not leave one stone
upon another in you, because you did not know the time of
your visitation."

Remember the language that Jesus used in Matthew 24 about God
not leaving one stone of the temple upon another? Well, he used it here
again, linking those two prophecies about the destruction that was
coming in AD 70. At that time, Titus had his army set up a barricade all
around Jerusalem, just as Jesus said they would. And just as Jesus had
prophesied, they subsequently tore down both city and temple to the
ground, not leaving one stone of that temple upon another.

Once again, Jesus makes clear that the reason for this judgment of
destruction upon the city and temple was because its Jewish residents
"did not know the time of your visitation" (v 44). That visitation was
the visitation of God himself incarnate in the Messiah (Luke 1:68; 7:16).
This first-century judgment for rejecting Messiah turns out to be a major
motif of Jesus's own ministry (Matthew 11:16-18; 12:39-42; 21:33-45;
23:29-39; Mark 8:38-9:1).

The abomination that brought desolation to Jerusalem and the
temple is not a prophecy of our future but a fulfillment in our past. It
was the Roman ruler Titus Vespasian and his pagan armies who would
defile the holy place and destroy both temple and holy city in AD 70,
thereby fulfilling Daniel's prophecy.

> Daniel 9:26–27
> And the people of the prince who is to come shall destroy
> the city and the sanctuary. Its end shall come with a flood,
> and to the end there shall be war. Desolations are
> decreed.... And on the wing of abominations shall come
> one who makes desolate, until the decreed end is poured
> out on the desolate.

I am very aware that applying the abomination of desolation in Daniel
12 to Titus in AD 70 will offend some futuristic prophecy schemes and
scenarios. As I have already indicated, there are many questions to be

answered about the rest of Daniel's prophecies, but this booklet is a vanguard for addressing those issues by starting with the immediate context around the abomination of desolation before working outward to the rest of the story. The reader can pursue a fuller treatment in my teaching videos called <u>Daniel and End Times Prophecy</u>.

What About the Image of the Beast?

Another question may arise in the mind of the Christian who has a futurist orientation in their prophecy system. What about Revelation 13? That passage talks about the Land Beast creating an image of the Sea Beast for the people to worship. Isn't that the abomination of desolation that Jesus was talking about?

> Revelation 13:14–15
> [The land beast told the people] to make an image for the [sea] beast that was wounded by the sword and yet lived. And it was allowed to give breath to the image of the beast, so that the image of the beast might even speak and might cause those who would not worship the image of the beast to be slain.

Though this passage is certainly about idolatrous worship of an image, there is no connection to the abomination in Daniel or Jesus. First, the words abomination and desolation are nowhere mentioned or even hinted at. This is a minimum requirement if one is to make a connection to such a particular prophecy.

Second, this beastly image is not said to have any relation to the Jerusalem temple whatsoever, which is a key part of the definition of the biblical abomination of desolation. Some believe this image is placed in the temple, but that is an assumption simply not in the text. This is commonly called eisegesis when a person imposes their own extrabiblical system upon the text in order to keep their system from falling apart.

Third, the existence of an idolatrous image in a text does not automatically connect it to the abomination of desolation predicted by Daniel or Jesus. There are multiple places in the Old Testament where abominable images of Asherah and other Canaanite deities are spoken of being in the temple (2 Kings 21:4-7; 23:6). Any time an idol is brought into God's house, it could be accused of being an abomination. Though one could fairly call them abominations of desolation *by way of analogy*, one could never call them *the* abomination of desolation spoken of by Daniel and Jesus.

Of course, addressing Revelation further takes us far afield of the purpose of this examination. Many believe Revelation to be a prophecy about our future. But see my podcast series Revelation & End Times Bible Prophecy[24] for a detailed exegesis of Revelation as a prophecy about the first-century judgment of Jesus Christ upon Jerusalem and the temple with the coming of the new covenant kingdom of God. Or read my novel series Chronicles of the Apocalypse for the narrative telling of that story in the first century: the origin of the book of Revelation. Shocking to those who have been taught a futurist paradigm as if it were the only orthodox option. Shocking but more biblical.

•••••

Chart of the Syrian Wars in Daniel 11

Here is a chart of the possible fulfillment of the Syrian Wars of the Greek third kingdom in the prophecies of Daniel.[25]

---

24 https://www.youtube.com/playlist?list=PL5TyMLcYh4AOz1_nbyeMQCQWW7pk097sG

25 I have drawn much of the information in this chart from: Jay Rogers, *In the Days of These Kings: The Book of Daniel in Preterist Perspective* (Clermont, FL: Media House International, 2017), and Philip Mauro, *The Seventy Weeks and the Great Tribulation: A Study of the Last Two Visions of Daniel, and of the Olivet Discourse of the Lord Jesus Christ* (Public Domain, 1921, 1944), and Bruce Gore's teaching "Antiochus Epiphanes and the Maccabees," https://www.youtube.com/watch?v=6hwkThHYBXs

Daniel Citation	Text or Symbols	Fulfillment
8:5-8, 21-22	Male goat and great horn	Alexander the Great
8:8, 22	Four horns from the broken great horn	The four kings that split up the empire after Alexander's death: Ptolemy (Egypt), Seleucus (Persia), Antigonis (Asia Minor), and Cassander (Macedon)
8:9, 23-26	Little horn grows exceedingly great toward the glorious land	Antiochus IV Epiphanes (Seleucid) turns his attention to Jerusalem
8:11-12	Burnt offering and sanctuary overthrown	Antiochus IV defiling the temple with a statue of Zeus and pig offering
11:3-4	A mighty king to arise	Alexander the Great
11:4	Kingdom divided to the four winds of heaven	The four kings that split up the empire after Alexander's death
Chapter 11	King of the South	Ptolemaic kings of Egypt
Chapter 11	King of the North	Seleucid kings of Syria/Babylon
11:5-6	North-South alliance	First Syrian War: Ptolemy II of Egypt vs. Antiochus I of Seleucia; Antiochus II marries Ptolemy's daughter Berenice in alliance
11:7-9	A branch arises in the South and attacks the fortress of the North	Ptolemy III arises when his sister Berenice is murdered and makes war on Seleucus II of Syria; Ptolemy occupies Antioch in Syria
11:10-12	Sons of the King of the North wage war on the King of the South	Fourth Syrian War: Sons of Seleucus, Seleucus III Soter and Antiochus III the Great, attack Ptolemy IV Philopater of Egypt
11:13-18	The King of the North raises a multitude	Fifth Syrian War: Ptolemy IV dies and Antiochus III attacks Syria to regain; includes either the battle of Panium or battle of Sidon
11:17-19	"shall give him the daughter"	Antiochus III gives his daughter Cleopatra I to Ptolemy V in a peace treaty
11:21	"And in his place a despicable person will arise on whom they have not conferred the majesty of the kingdom, and he will come in without warning and he will seize the kingdom by deceit."	175 BC; Antiochus IV is the despicable one who was not next in line for kingship; he claims to rule on behalf of Demetrius, the heir, while Demetrius is in Rome as hostage

11:23	"After an alliance is made with him he will practice deception, and he will go up and gain power with a small force of people."	After Antiochus IV gets his small military force in place, he disavows Demetrius as heir and takes the throne for himself
11:22	"The overflowing forces will be flooded away before him and shattered, and also the prince of the covenant."	Sixth Syrian War: Antiochus IV comes to power and attacks both the Jews and Ptolemy VI of Egypt; the prince of the covenant may be the righteous high priest Onias III
11:24	"In a time of tranquility he will enter the richest parts of the realm, and he will accomplish what his fathers never did, nor his ancestors; he will distribute plunder, booty and possessions among them, and he will devise his schemes against strongholds, but only for a time."	Antiochus IV uses his wealth to buy loyalty in the Syrian provinces; he plunders temples, including the temple in Jerusalem, and plans a campaign against Egypt in the South; through the new high priest Jason, Antiochus Hellenizes Jerusalem, leading to the Maccabean Revolt
11:25-26	"He will stir up his strength and courage against the king of the South with a large army; so the king of the South will mobilize an extremely large and mighty army for war; but he will not stand, for schemes will be devised against him. Those who eat his choice food will destroy him, and his army will overflow, but many will fall down slain."	170 BC; Antiochus IV angers the King of the South, Ptolemy VI, and sends his army toward Syria, but Antiochus ambushes the Egyptian forces at Pelusium and takes much of Egypt, except for Alexandria; Ptolemy becomes his puppet king
11:27	"As for both kings, their hearts will be intent on evil, and they will speak lies to each other at the same table; but it will not succeed, for the end is still to come at the appointed time."	Two Ptolemys now rule Egypt together: Ptolemy VIII governs Alexandria while Ptolemy VI governs the rest of Egypt
11:28	"Then he will return to his land with much plunder; but his heart will be set against the holy covenant, and he will take action and then return to his own land."	169 BC; Antiochus IV leaves Egypt and returns to Syria with his Egyptian plunder; he stops at Jerusalem and sacks it for gold and silver
11:29-30	"At the appointed time he will return and come into the South, but this last time it will not turn out the way it did before. For ships of Kittim will	168 BC; Antiochus IV returns to invade Egypt a second time and take Alexandria but Rome stops him ("Kittim")

	come against him; therefore he will be disheartened and will return and become enraged at the holy covenant and take action; so he will come back and show regard for those who forsake the holy covenant."	Antiochus returns to Syria but again becomes enraged at a civil war that has begun in Jerusalem, prompting him to attack Jerusalem
11:31	"Forces from him will arise, desecrate the sanctuary fortress, and do away with the regular sacrifice. And they will set up the abomination of desolation."	167 BC; Antiochus IV halts the daily sacrifices and sacrifices a pig to Zeus on the altar; forces the Jews to forsake their covenant obedience by eating swine and not observing circumcision, dietary laws, or the Sabbath
11:32-35	"By smooth words he will turn to godlessness those who act wickedly toward the covenant, but the people who know their God will display strength and take action...Some of those who have insight will fall, in order to refine, purge and make them pure until the end time; because it is still to come at the appointed time."	Hellenist Jews are seduced to give up their obedience to the Mosaic covenant. But... 165 BC; the Maccabean Revolt against Antiochus IV results in many martyrs; the Maccabees successfully force the Seleucids out of Jerusalem, cleanse the temple, and resumes the Mosaic sacrifices
11:36-45	The Willful King who exalts himself against God and also enters glorious land rules at the time of the end	1st century BC; probably Herod the Great, but some argue for Julius Caesar and the line of Caesars, Titus, or (least likely) Antiochus IV

• • • • •

If you liked this book, then please help me out by writing a positive review of it on Amazon. That is one of the best ways to say thank you to me as an author. It really does help my sales and status. Thanks!—*Brian Godawa*

More Books by Brian Godawa

See www.Godawa.com for more information on other books by Brian Godawa. Check out his other series below.

Chronicles of the Nephilim

Chronicles of the Nephilim is a saga that charts the rise and fall of the Nephilim giants of Genesis 6 and their place in the evil plans of the fallen angelic Sons of God called "The Watchers." The story starts in the days of

Enoch and continues on through the Bible until the arrival of the Messiah, Jesus. The prelude to Chronicles of the Apocalypse. ChroniclesOfTheNephilim.com. (affiliate link)

Chronicles of the Apocalypse

Chronicles of the Apocalypse is an origin story of the most controversial book of the Bible: Revelation. A historical conspiracy thriller series in first century Rome set against the backdrop of explosive spiritual warfare of Satan and his demonic Watchers. ChroniclesOfTheApocalypse.com. (affiliate link)

Chronicles of the Watchers

Chronicles of the Watchers is a series that charts the influence of spiritual principalities and powers over the course of human history. The kingdoms of man in service to the gods of the nations at war. Completely based on ancient historical and mythological research. ChroniclesOfTheWatchers.com. (affiliate link)

Get the novel set
Judah Maccabee: Parts 1&2
based on the biblical research of this book you are reading.

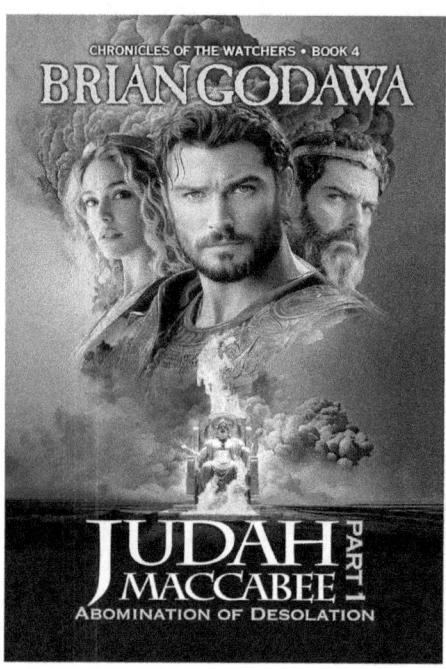
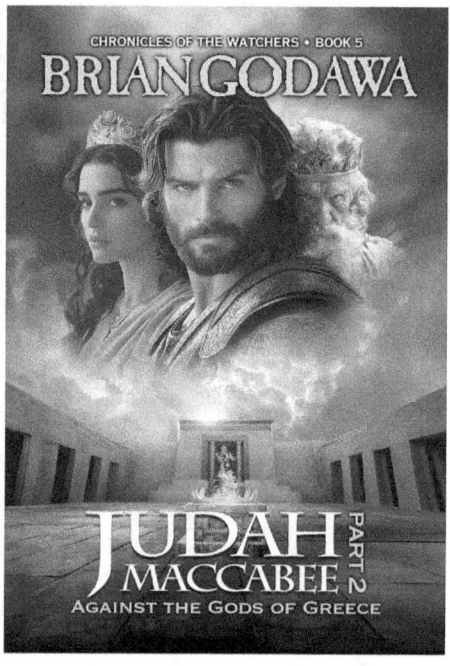

The Supernatural Story of Hanukkah and the Abomination of Desolation.

An epic action Bible novel about the most important Jewish story between the Old and New Testaments, the story of the Maccabees. Respected Christian author Brian Godawa reveals the spiritual realm like never before in this biblically faithful spiritual warfare novel.

https://godawa.com/get-judah-part-1/

(affiliate link)

Great Offers By Brian Godawa

Get More
Biblical Imagination
Sign up Online For The Godawa Chronicles
www.Godawa.com

Updates and Freebies
of the Books of Brian Godawa
Special Discounts, Weird Bible Facts!

About the Author

Brian Godawa is a respected Christian writer and best-selling author of novels and biblical theology. His supernatural Bible epic novels combine creative imagination with orthodox Christian theology in a way that transcends both entertainment and preachiness.

His love for Jesus and storytelling was forged in the crucible of worldview apologetics and Hollywood screenwriting, as he began a career in movies and eventually expanded into the world of novels.

His first novel series, *Chronicles of the Nephilim* has been in the Top 10 of Biblical Fiction on Amazon for more than a decade, selling over 350,000 books. His popular book *Hollywood Worldviews: Watching Films with Wisdom and Discernment* is used as a textbook in Christian film schools around the country. His movies *To End All Wars* and *Alleged* have won multiple movie awards such as Cannes Film Festival and the Heartland International Film Festival.

He lives in Texas with the most amazing wife a man could ever pray for and is accountable to a local church. He reads too many books and watches too many movies. He knows, he knows, he should get out more.

Find out more about his blog and his other books, lectures, and online courses for sale at his website, www.godawa.com.

BLANK PAGE

BLANK PAGE

BLANK PAGE

BLANK PAGE

BLANK PAGE

BLANK PAGE

BLANK PAGE

BLANK PAGE

www.ingramcontent.com/pod-product-compliance
Lightning Source LLC
Chambersburg PA
CBHW071538120626
46550CB00006B/2499